OXFORD PRACTICE TESTS

Age 13-14

SCIENCE

Practice Tests
for Key Stage 3

SCIENCE

Sheila Dampney and John Aldridge

OXFORD

OXFORD
UNIVERSITY PRESS

Great Clarendon Street, Oxford OX2 6DP

Oxford University Press is a department of the University of Oxford.
It furthers the University's objective of excellence in research, scholarship,
and education by publishing worldwide in

Oxford New York

Athens Auckland Bangkok Bogotá Buenos Aires Calcutta
Cape Town Chennai Dar es Salaam Delhi Florence Hong Kong Istanbul
Karachi Kuala Lumpur Madrid Melbourne Mexico City Mumbai
Nairobi Paris São Paulo Singapore Taipei Tokyo Toronto Warsaw

with associated companies in Berlin Ibadan

Oxford is a registered trade mark of Oxford University Press
in the UK and in certain other countries

About the authors
Sheila Dampney has taught science for over twenty years. Currently Senior Lecturer in Science
and Education at St Mary's University College in Twickenham; John Aldridge has over twenty
years experience of developing educational assessment materials.

Acknowledgements
Sally Aston at St Mary's University College, for editorial assistance, Ian Dampney,
David Aldridge at Chiswick Community School

Photo acknowledgements: The Image Bank p19; Aldridge Archive

First published 1999

ISBN 0 19 838248 0

Packaged by Aldridge Press
Designed by Geoffrey Wadsley
Edited by Angela Royston
Illustrations by Maureen and Gordon Gray pp16, 47, 52; John and Jane Booth the remainder
Typeset in Garth Graphic
Printed in Hong Kong

Contents

It has been shown that practising for National Tests (formerly called SATs) improves a student's scores. This book provides tests for levels 4 to 7 at Key Stage 3. The average student gains level 5, while the majority (about 75 per cent) gain level 4, 5 or 6. A further 10 per cent gain level 7. This book provides:

1 practice tests for science at Key Stage 3
2 a method of assessing the level you are currently working at and help in diagnosing the topics you need to study further
3 an index of topics to help you revise

Tiers and levels in National Tests

The National Test papers that you take in May are arranged in tiers and are designed to cover a range of abilities. Your teacher will decide which of two tiers you will sit: level 3-6 or level 5-7. Each tier consists of two one-hour written test papers: Paper 1 and Paper 2. Both Papers include questions on:

Life processes and living things ('Biology');
Materials and their properties ('Chemistry');
Physical processes ('Physics').

In addition, your teacher will assess your levels of attainment in *Experimental and investigative science* from the coursework you do during the year.

If your teacher estimates that you are really excellent at science, you will be asked to take an extra 'extension' paper to assess whether you are at level 8 or higher.

Test practice papers

This book contains six practice tests. There are two tests at each of levels 4–5, levels 5–6 and levels 6–7. Read the paragraph on marking the tests before trying the second test at any level. Every question tells you what topic is being assessed; this will aid your revision.

Practising skills

In the National Test papers the questions are often put into a situation you may be unfamiliar with. Don't panic! Read the question carefully and think through the question – you may well be able to answer it. The tests in this book provide practice in the skills you will need to answer the questions. The questions in the National Tests will provide opportunities for you to show those skills.

Before you start a test

1 Make sure you have a quiet place to work where you will not be disturbed.
2 Have some spare paper beside you in case you need more space to note your ideas.
3 Make a note of the time you start and set an alarm to warn you when you must finish.

Time allowed for each test

Give yourself 30 minutes for each test. If at the end of 30 minutes you have not completed the test, make a note of where you got to and carry on with the rest of the test. When you assess your level only count the marks you scored during the first half hour.

Marking the tests

Use the answer pages to mark each test. The wording of your answer may not be exactly the same as that given. Alternative wording is often given, but if your answer differs, think about it carefully. Make sure that your answer contains all the points covered before you give yourself a mark. If your answer is incomplete or wrong, think about the question carefully. Did you make a careless mistake or do you not fully understand the topic?

Help

Many answers provide extra information to help you understand the question and answer better. Read the help paragraphs carefully: they can help you gain extra marks in the National Tests. If you are still unclear or confused about the question and answer, ask your teacher or use revision guides for extra help with the topic. The title of the question tells you which topic to look up and revise further and/or ask for help with.

Assessing your level

Each test has 45 points. If you scored:

25 points or less – You still have a lot of work to do at this level.
26–37 points – Pick out the topics you have found difficult and do more work on them.
38 points or more – Well done, you will most likely pass at this level.

If you get less than 38 in the first test at a level, do some more work – especially on those topics where you have made mistakes – before attempting the second test. When you have completed each two tests at the same levels, turn to page 64. Add your two totals together and fill in the scale for the two tests you have just done. Now you can see what level you have achieved in these practice tests.

For each level on the scale you can achieve the following three sub-levels of attainment. These mean, for example:

Good Level 5 – You should achieve this level. Well done! Try next time for level 6...
Working at Level 5 – You might achieve this level, but you had better do more revision.
Working towards Level 5 – Better get working! Lots of revision to do to achieve this level.

Revision

The index on pages 62 and 63 shows you at a glance which topics are covered at key stage 3. These are arranged under the following three main headings:

1 Life processes and living things
2 Materials and their properties
3 Physical processes

You can use this list as a revision checklist. It also shows which tests include a question on any particular topic. The practice tests concentrate on the topics which are most likely to come up in the National Tests so not every topic has a question on it in this book.

If you achieved the top level for the tests, go on to the next set of tests, but, when starting a new set, do not expect necessarily to pass it first time. This book helps you to improve and practise your skills so that you will do better next time – and surprise your parents and teachers... and even yourself!

	Time started	:
• Test 1 •	Time finished	:

Earth in space

LEVEL 4

1 Class 8W are designing a sundial.
They are investigating the position and length of the shadows formed by a shadow stick at different times of the day.

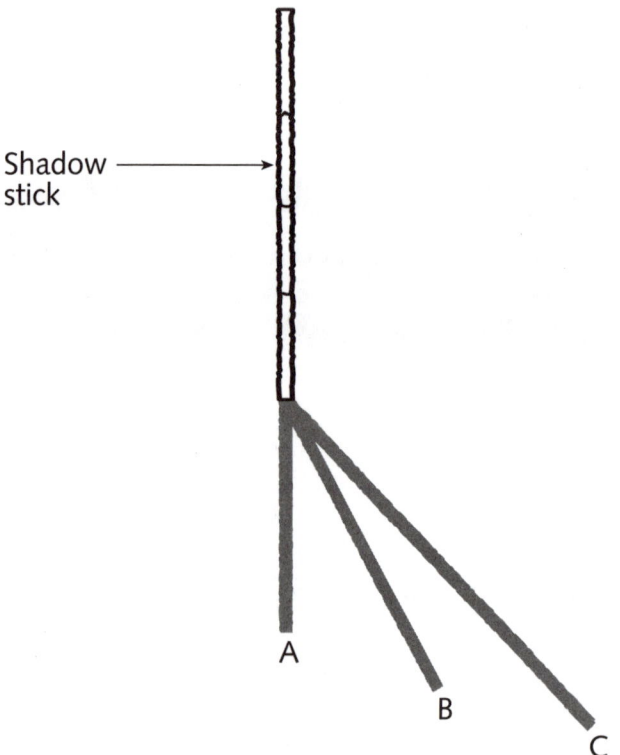

Shadow stick

A

B

C

They have recorded three measurements.

a Complete the table below to show the times the measurements were made at A, B and C.

Time of measurement	Position of shadow
9.00am	
10.30am	
12.00 noon	

b Draw a line on the shadow stick diagram above to show the length and position of the shadow at 3.00pm.

PAGE TOTAL

■■■ *Earth in space*   LEVEL 4

c   **Explain why the Sun appears to change position during the day.**

_____

_____

_____

☐

d   **In which direction is the Sun positioned in Britain at noon?**

_____

☐

e   **Use some of these words to fill in the blanks to explain why the shadow stick forms a shadow on a sunny day.**

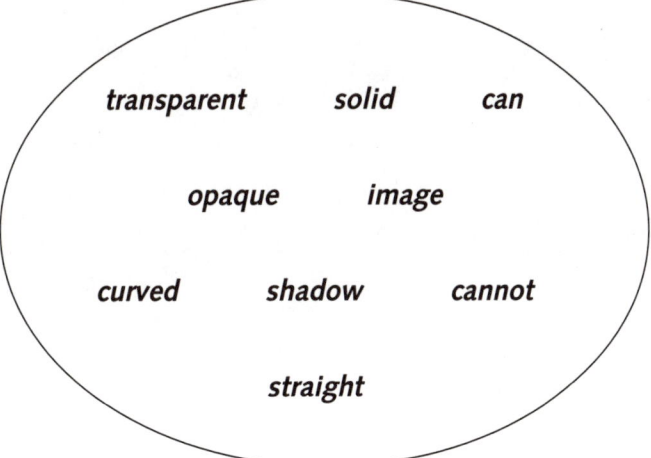

transparent   solid   can

opaque   image

curved   shadow   cannot

straight

The shadow stick is made from _____ material. The light from the   ☐

Sun travels in _____ lines and _____ pass through this   ☐ ☐

material and so a _____ is formed.   ☐

PAGE
TOTAL

Acids and Alkalis

2

Litmus is a dye produced from lichen. Litmus paper is used as an indicator to test for acids and alkalis.

a   **Complete the chart below to show what happened to red and blue litmus paper when these bathroom products were tested. One has been done for you.**

	Red Litmus	Blue Litmus	Acid/Alkali/Neutral
shower gel (with pH 5.5)			acid
pure water	stays red	stays blue	neutral
liquid soap			alkali
bathroom cleaner with limescale remover.		turns red	

Indigestion is caused by excess acid in the stomach. Indigestion tablets are alkaline.

b   **What is the process called when an acid reacts with an alkali to form a neutral solution?**

_____

PAGE TOTAL

■■■■ *Acids and Alkalis*   LEVEL 4

c

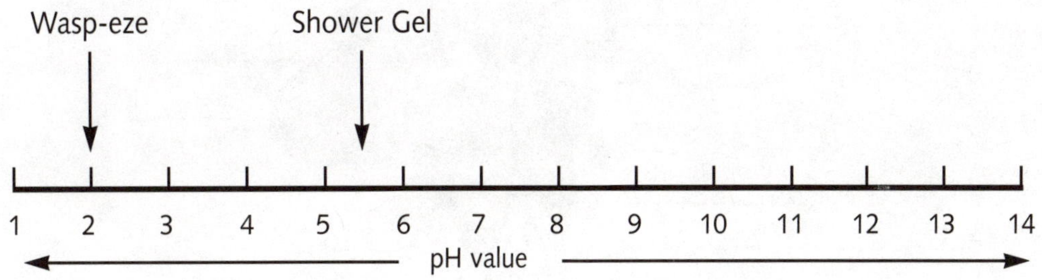

Wasp-eze   Shower Gel

1   2   3   4   5   6   7   8   9   10   11   12   13   14
                        pH value

The chart shows the pH scale. The pH value of Shower Gel and Wasp-eze are shown.

Use an arrow to show the pH value of pure water.

d   Wasp-eze has a pH value of 2. It is used to treat wasp stings.

What does this tell you about the pH value of a wasp sting?

_____

e   **What disadvantage does using litmus paper have when used as an indicator?**

_____

_____

_____

f   **What advantage does using a universal indicator have over using litmus paper?**

_____

_____

PAGE
TOTAL

Plants

3

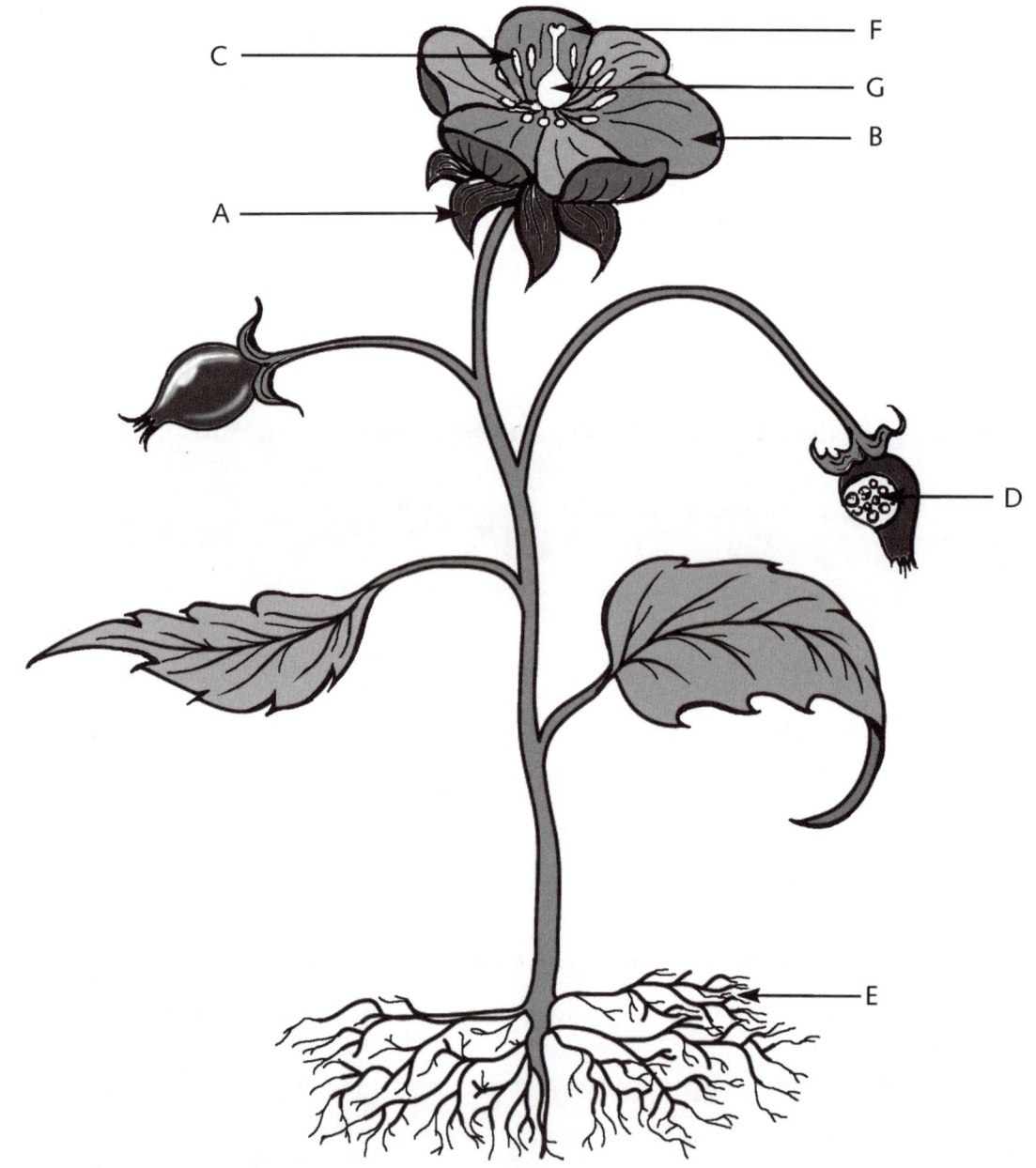

a   Match the letter to the part of the plant listed below. One has been done for you.

Part of the plant	Letter
sepal	A
petal	
fruit	
root	
stigma	
anther	
ovary	

PAGE TOTAL

■■■■ *Plants*   LEVEL 5

b   **Use arrows to join each part of the plant to its function. One has been done for you.**

Part of plant	Function
petal	produces male cell
stigma	attracts insects
sepal	absorbs water and minerals
ovary	protects developing flower
leaf	grows into new plant
root	receives pollen
anther	produces female cell
seed	makes food

c   **Fill in the gaps to complete the two sentences below.**

i)   When an insect visits a flower, _____pollen_____ is deposited on the

_____ . This is known as _____ .

ii)   The pollen grain may grow a tube down to the ovary.

The _____ cell passes down the tube and fuses with the

_____ cell. This is known as _____ .

PAGE
TOTAL

Habitat

4

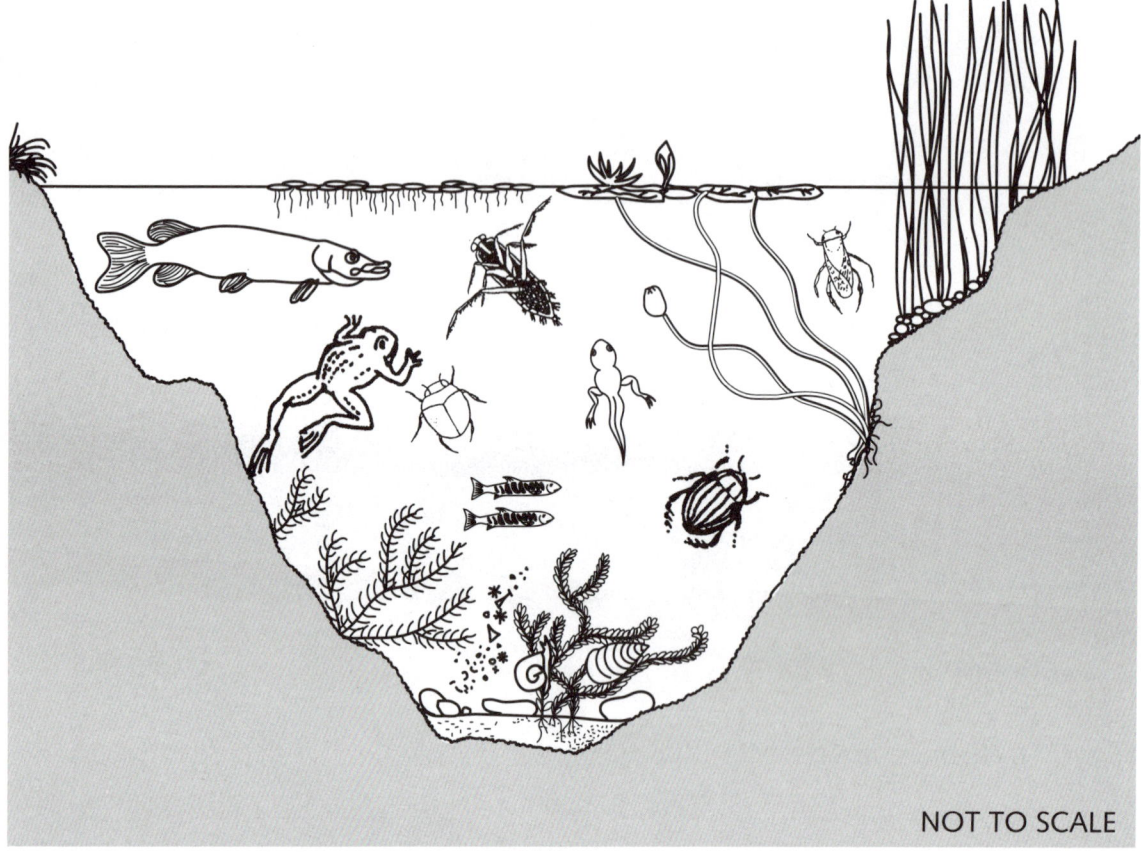

NOT TO SCALE

Tadpoles feed on duckweed.
Pike eat water beetles.
Tadpoles are eaten by water beetles.

a   **Write this as a food chain.**

_____

b   i)   Name the producer in this food chain: _____

ii)   Name the primary consumer in this food chain: _____

iii) Name a predator in this food chain: _____

c   **Fishing reduces the pike population greatly. What effect would this
reduction have, if any, on the number of tadpoles?**

_____

_____

PAGE
TOTAL

Light

5   **a**   Joan and Alan are carrying out light experiments in a *darkened* room.

Draw arrows on the picture to show how Alan sees the cardboard tube when Joan switches on the torch.

PAGE
TOTAL

■ ■ ■ *Light*

b   Joan shone a torch down the cardboard tube onto a mirror.
Alan was trying to see the light in the torch by looking down a second tube.

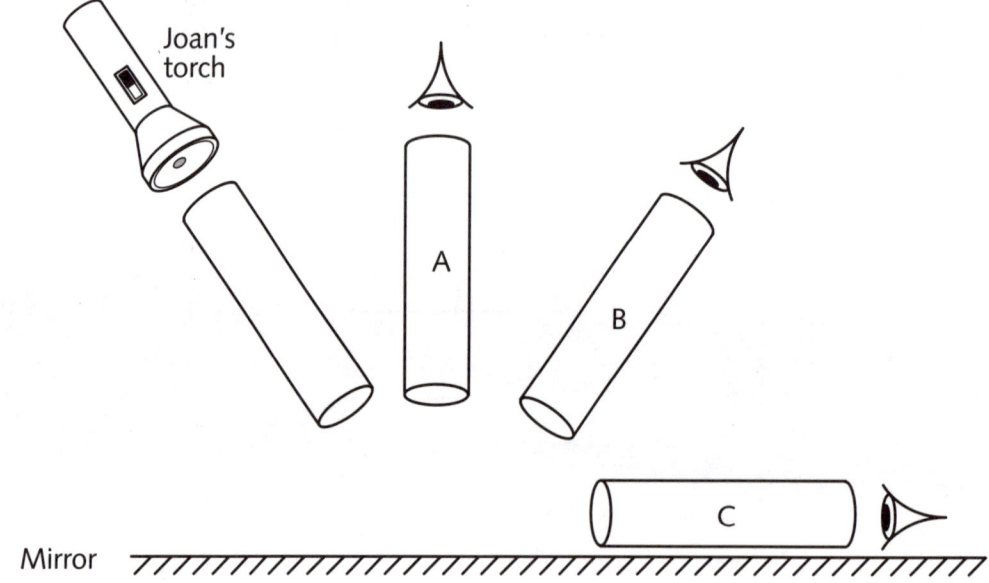

Mirror

Tick the box to show where he saw the light from the torch:

i)   position A   ☐

ii) position B   ☐

iii) position C   ☐

c   **Draw arrows to show how the light behaves when it hits**

i)   a smooth surface   ii)   a rough surface

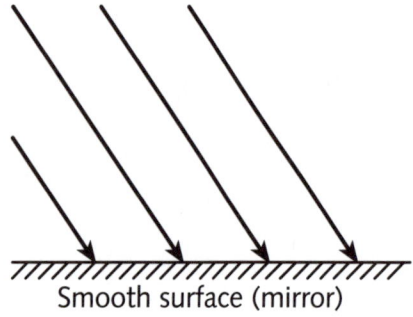

Smooth surface (mirror)

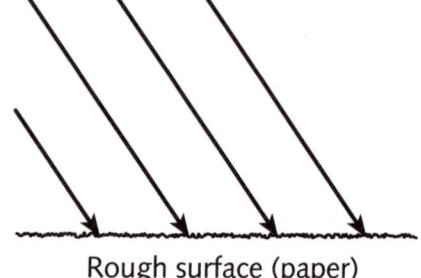

Rough surface (paper)

PAGE
TOTAL

<table>
<tr><td></td><td>Time started</td><td>:</td></tr>
<tr><td>• **Test 2** •</td><td>Time finished</td><td>:</td></tr>
</table>

The human body

LEVEL 5

1

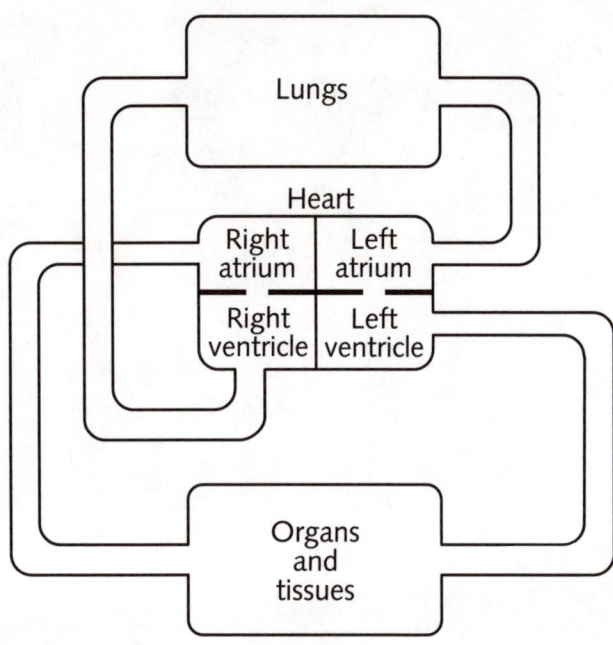

a   Use the diagram above to help you to complete these sentences.

The diagram shows the _____ system in the human body.   ☐

The right side of the heart receives _____ blood and pumps   ☐

it to the _____ .   ☐

The left side of the heart pumps _____ blood to the   ☐

_____ .   ☐

_____ carry blood to the heart.   ☐

b   Name two main functions of blood in the human body.

i)   _____

_____   ☐

ii)   _____

_____   ☐

PAGE
TOTAL

Changing materials

2

Today we are going to investigate how to make a quick cup of tea.

Saman and Alistair predict that caster sugar would be 'better' to add to the tea.

a   Their teacher asks them to explain what they mean by 'better'.
Tick one box to explain 'better' in a scientific way.

	It melts first
	It is sweeter
	It dissolves more easily
	It disappears the quickest

PAGE TOTAL

■■■ *Changing materials* LEVEL 4

b They design a chart to record the results of their test.

Type of sugar	Number of stirs

> **i) What did they *change* in each test?**

_____ ☐

> **ii) What did they *measure* in each test?**

_____ ☐

c They used the same type of tea bags each time and placed the container in the same location.

> **Name three more things they must keep the same to make the test fair.**

i) _____ ☐

ii) _____ ☐

iii) _____ ☐

d **Their teacher asked them to write a report of their test using correct scientific vocabulary. Choose from these words to complete the sentences they wrote.**

soluble   solvent   solute   insoluble

saturated   soaked   dissolved   solution

We sprinkled the sugar (the _____) into the tea (the _____)
to form a _____ . The sugar _____ .   ☐ ☐
We concluded that caster sugar was more _____ in tea than   ☐ ☐
granulated sugar.   ☐

Electricity

3

Red

Amber

Green

a   Alice is designing some traffic lights for Will's car track.

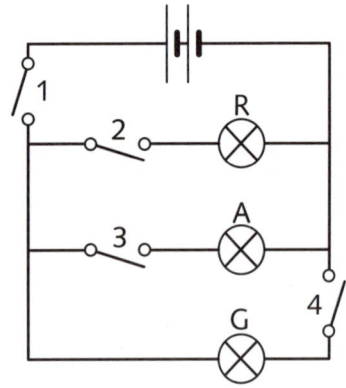

She closes
all the
switches:

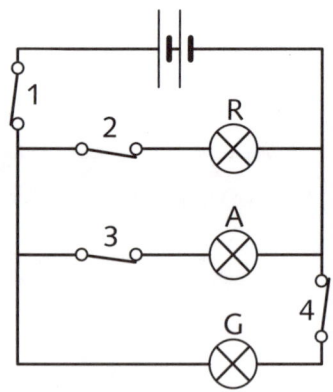

i)   **Tick the boxes to show which lamp, if any, will light up when she *only opens switch 4*.**

Ⓡ ☐
Ⓐ ☐
Ⓖ ☐

ii) **Tick the boxes to show which lamp, if any, will light up when she *only opens switch 1*.**

Ⓡ ☐
Ⓐ ☐
Ⓖ ☐

iii) **Tick the boxes to show the switches she must open for *only the green lamp* to light up.**

1 ☐
2 ☐
3 ☐
4 ☐

b   Alice wants to produce a chart to help Will operate his traffic lights.

Complete the chart below to show which switches he must close for the lamps to shine.

How to make the traffic lights work *Close the switches shown*				
	1	**2**	**3**	**4**
Ⓡ				
Ⓡ + Ⓐ				
Ⓖ				
Ⓐ				

PAGE
TOTAL

Light and Sound

LEVEL 5

4

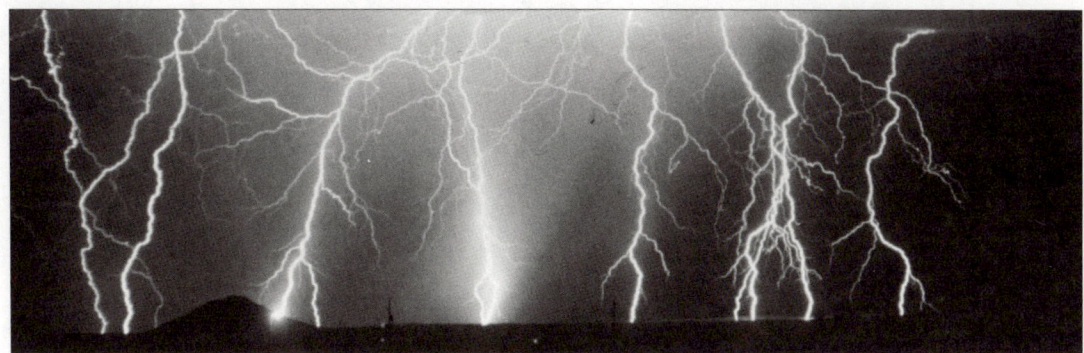

Both light and sound travel in waves.

a   Tick the boxes to show what light and sound can each do.

	Light	Sound
Travel through air		
Travel through a vacuum		
Travel through wood		
Travel through water		
Travel in all directions from a source		
Can be reflected off hard surfaces		

b   You see lightning in the night sky. Six seconds later you hear thunder.

Explain why there is a delay in your observations.

_____

c   As the storm continues, the delay between seeing the lightning and hearing the thunder decreases.

i)   Tick one box to show what happens to the sound of thunder.

The thunder is quieter than before	
The thunder is louder than before	
The thunder sounds the same	

ii) What does this tell you about the storm?

_____

PAGE
TOTAL

Classification

5 These pictures show some common garden creatures.

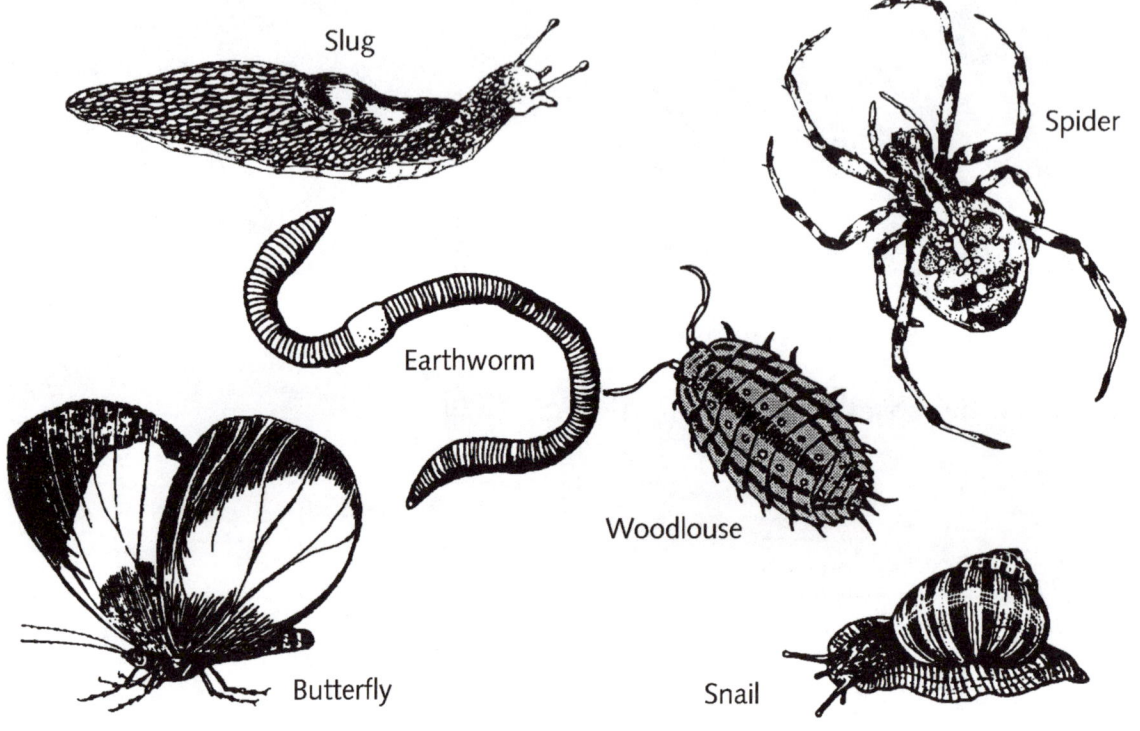

Slug

Spider

Earthworm

Woodlouse

Butterfly

Snail

NOT TO SCALE

a **Complete the branching key to identify the six garden creatures by providing statements for A, B, C and D.**

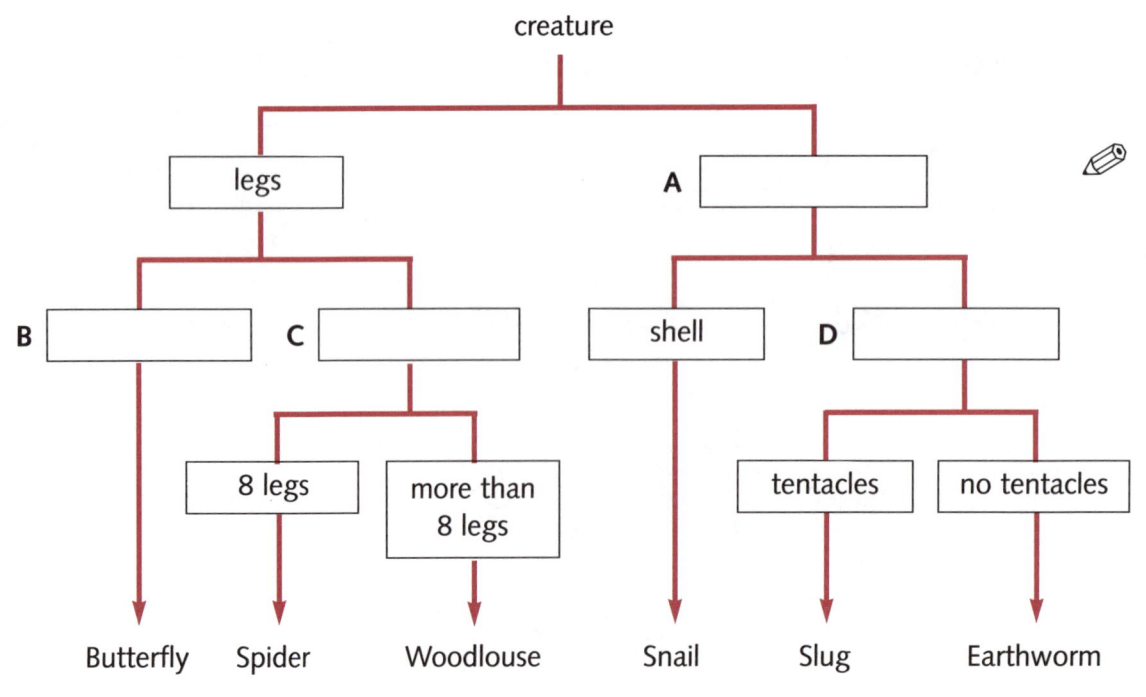

creature

legs

A

B

C

shell

D

8 legs

more than 8 legs

tentacles

no tentacles

Butterfly   Spider   Woodlouse   Snail   Slug   Earthworm

PAGE
TOTAL

■ ■ ■ ■ *Classification*   LEVEL 4

b Use the numbered key below to identify these leaves. Write the correct name beside each letter.

A _____

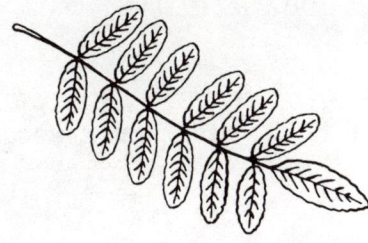

B _____

C _____

D _____

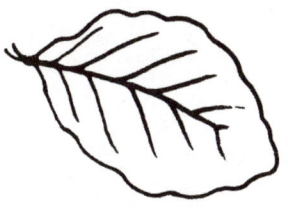

E _____

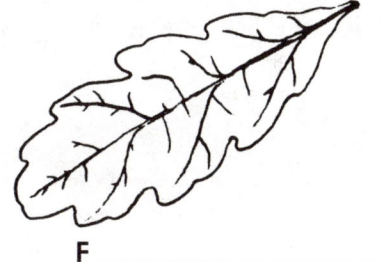

F _____

1	Leaf is one complete shape	go to 3
	Leaf is made from smaller leaflets	go to 2
2	Leaves are arranged either side of stem	ash
	Leaves arranged radically	horse-chestnut
3	There is one main leaf vein	go to 4
	There is more than one main leaf vein	sycamore
4	Leaves have serrated edges	lime
	Leaves have wavy edges	go to 5
5	Leaves are lobed	oak
	Leaves are not lobed	beech

PAGE TOTAL

Time started	:
Time finished	:

• Test 3 •

Separating mixtures

LEVEL 5

1 Recommend one way to separate each of the following mixtures of materials.

Mixture of materials	Way to separate
i) steel cans and aluminium cans	
ii) a mixture of sand and fine gravel	
iii) the pigments used in purple ink	
iv) a solution of salt and water	
v) a mixture of two powders, one of which dissolves in water	
vi) two immiscible liquids eg. oil and vinegar	

PAGE TOTAL

Variation

2

David is fourteen. He has short hair, **brown eyes**, **freckles** and a **long nose**.

He is **slim, 1.6m tall** and in his class at school he is average in height.

He is **intelligent**, an **excellent cyclist** and has a great sense of humour.

He speaks with a **London accent** and **loves to wear designer-label clothes**.

Read the description above of David.
Some of his features are written in bold.

Write these features in the correct column to show whether they are definitely inherited from his parents, definitely caused by environmental factors or a combination of both.

Definitely inherited	Definitely environmental	Both environmental and inherited
brown eyes		

PAGE TOTAL

Earth in space

3

The diagram below shows some positions of the Earth as it orbits the Sun.
* shows Britain.

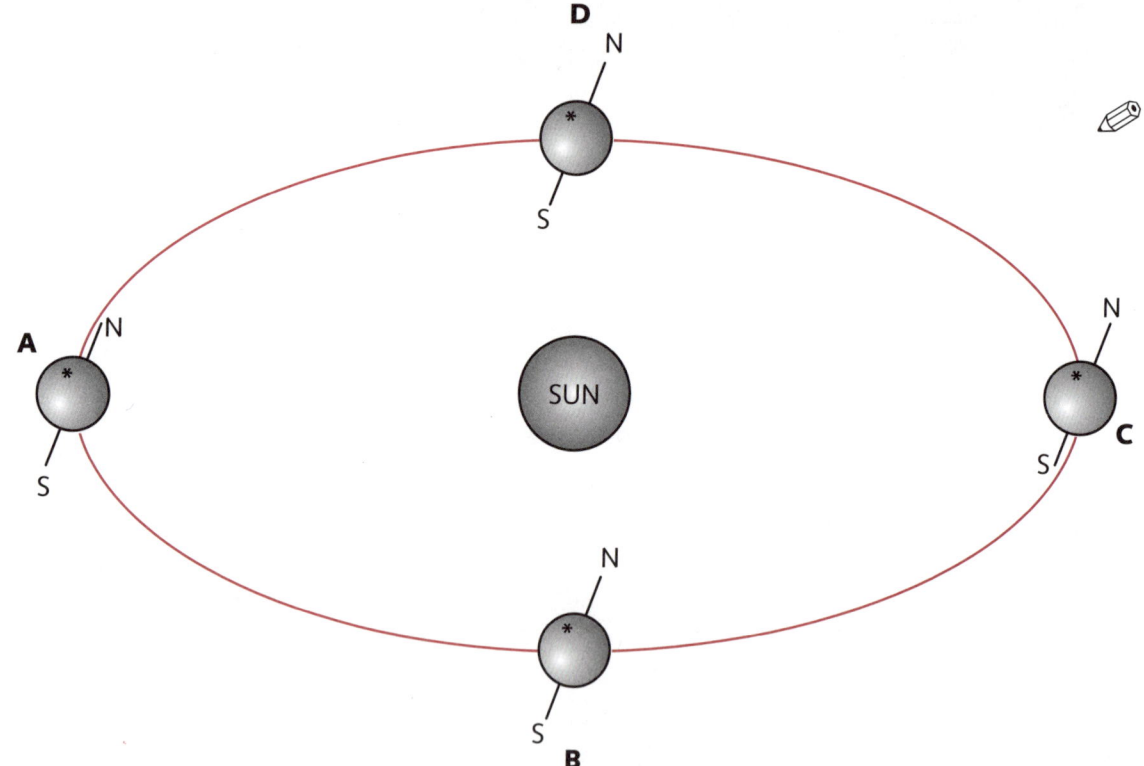

NOT TO SCALE

a   **How long does it take for the Earth to complete one orbit?**

_____

b   **Draw arrows on the diagram to show the direction of the Earth's orbit.**

PAGE
TOTAL

■■■ *Earth in space*

SUN

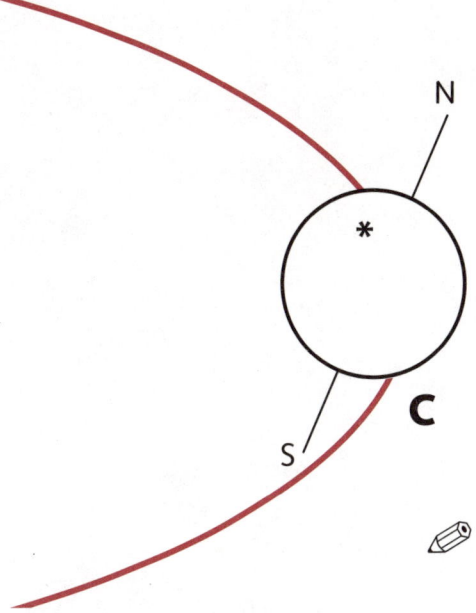

N

*

S

C

NOT TO SCALE

c   In position C, shade in the part of the Earth that is in darkness.

d   In position C, tick a box to show what time it is most likely to be in Britain.

0600		1300		0100		1700	

e   **i)**   Tick one box to show which season it is in the northern hemisphere when the Earth is in position A.

spring		summer		autumn		winter	

ii)   Tick one box to explain your answer.

	The Earth is nearer the Sun.
	The Earth is further away from the Sun.
	The Earth is tilted on its axis.
	The length of daytime and night time are equal.

PAGE TOTAL

The human body

4

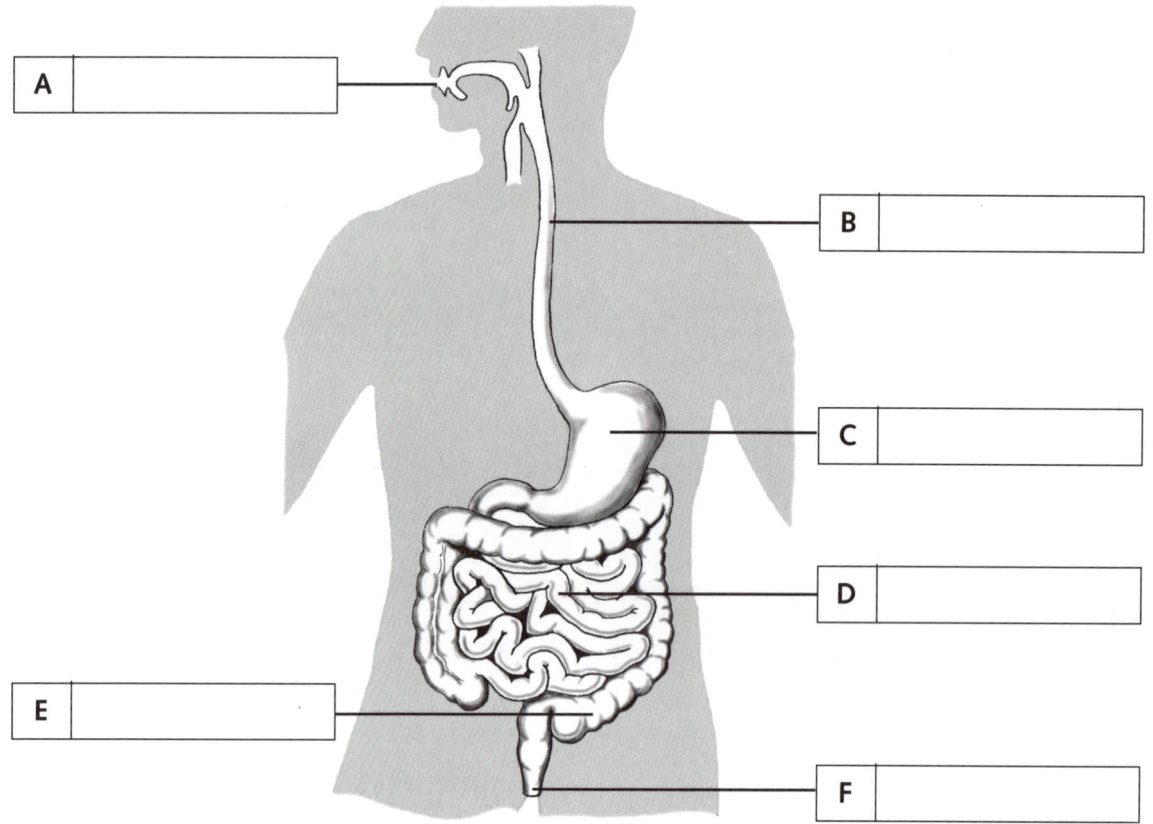

A

B

C

D

E

F

The diagram shows some major organs of the digestive system.

a   **Complete the labels A to F with the name of each part of the digestive system.**

b   **Use one of the letters A to F to describe the function of each part.**

Function	Part of digestive system
Absorbs water from undigested food	
Transports food to the stomach	
Absorbs digested food into the blood	
Starch starts to be broken down	
Undigested food is expelled	
Protein starts to be broken down	

PAGE
TOTAL

Energy resources

5 The chart below lists some different sources of energy.

Source of energy	Column 1 renewable	Column 2 non-renewable	Column 3 Sun is original source of energy
solar			
wind	✓		
coal			
gas			
nuclear			
oil			
hydro-electricity			

a   Tick a box in column 1 or 2 to show if the type of energy is *renewable* or *non-renewable*. One has been done for you.

b   Tick a box in column 3 if the Sun is the *original* source of energy.

PAGE TOTAL

| Test 4 | Time started | : |
| | Time finished | : |

Geological changes

1

a The chart below describes five different rock samples.

Tick one box for each sample to show whether the rock is:

i) igneous
ii) sedimentary
iii) metamorphic

	Appearance	Igneous	Sedimentary	Metamorphic
A	Made up of large crystals, very hard			
B	Some crystals, fairly hard, different layers			
C	Soft, crumbly, made from fine grains			
D	Microscopic particles, soft, has fossils			
E	Very small crystals, hard, smooth			

b Sample D contains fossils.

Which other rock sample could contain fossils?

_____

PAGE TOTAL

Geological changes ■■■

c   **Name two factors which contribute to the formation of metamorphic rocks.**

i) _____

ii) _____

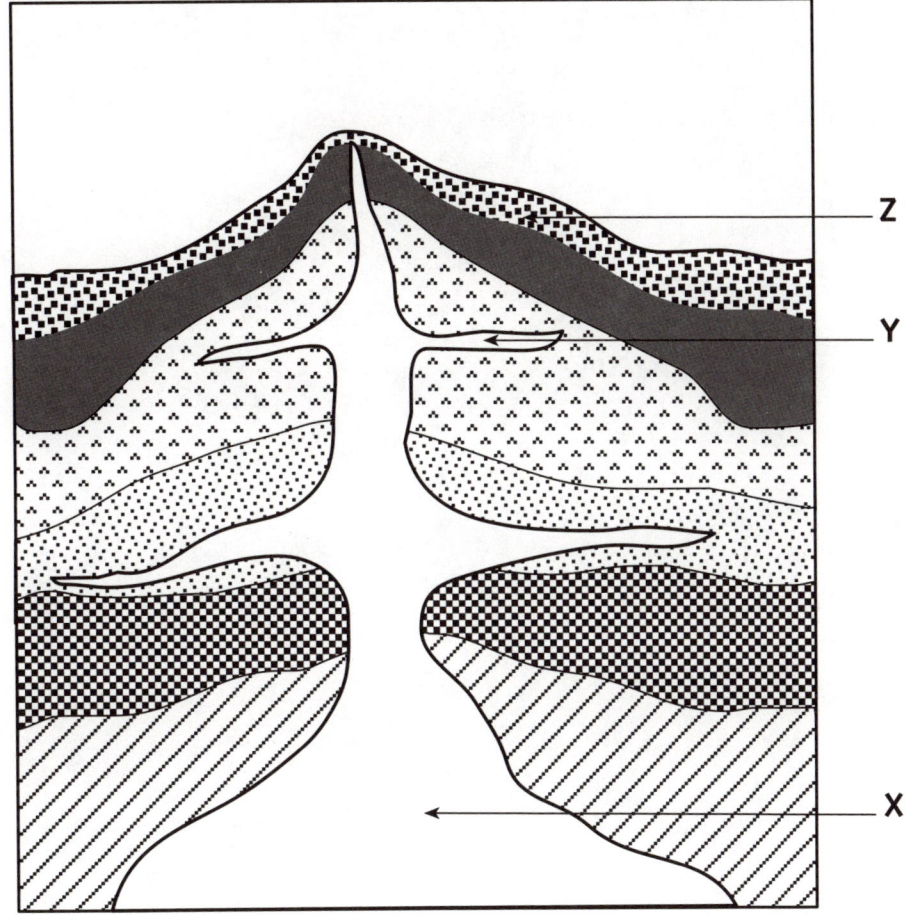

Z

Y

X

d   i) **Is rock A most likely to occur at position X, Y or Z?**

_____

ii) **Give a reason for your answer.**

_____

_____

_____

PAGE TOTAL

Forces

2 **a** A parachutist jumps from an aeroplane.
He *accelerates* as he starts his fall to Earth.

i) Draw arrows on the picture above to show the *direction* and *strength* of the two forces acting on him.

ii) How can we know the forces are not equal?

_____

PAGE
TOTAL

 *Forces*

b   He opens his parachute. He slows down and reaches a *steady* slower speed.

> **i)** Use arrows to show the *direction* and *strength* of forces acting on him now.

> **ii)** Name the force that causes him to fall to Earth.

_____

> **iii)** Name the force that slows him down.

_____

c   He lands on Earth and stops moving.
Draw arrows to show the forces acting on him now.

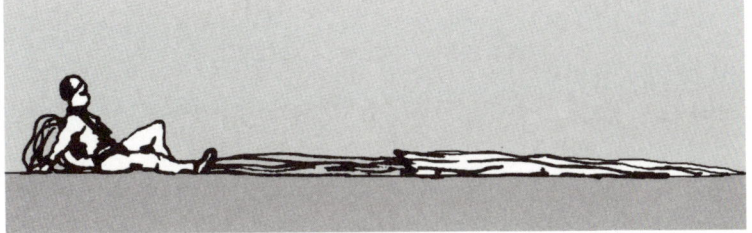

PAGE
TOTAL

Nutrition

3

Chicken and Cashew Nuts with Egg Fried Rice

Nutrition information per 100g	
Protein	26g
Carbohydrate	38.5g
Fat	15.6g
Fibre	2.5g
Sodium (minerals)	2.2g

Ingredients
chicken
brown rice
nuts
peas
red peppers
spring onions
salt
sunflower oil
egg

The nutrition information chart shows the main types of food in the meal.

a   **What food type essential for good health is missing from the nutrition information?**

_____

PAGE TOTAL

 *Nutrition*

LEVEL 6

b   Name two ingredients in the meal which are high in protein.

i) _____

ii) _____

c   Why is fibre important in a healthy diet?

_____

_____

d   Name three ingredients in the meal which have a high fibre content.

i) _____

ii) _____

iii) _____

e   Match some of the food types listed in the nutrition information chart to their use.

Food type	Use to the body
	provides energy
	for growth and repair
	storing energy

PAGE TOTAL

Materials

4

Sandeep noticed that some parts of his bike's frame were rusting.

He carried out a test to see what caused rusting to occur.

He placed six *identical* iron nails in different beakers as shown in the diagrams below.

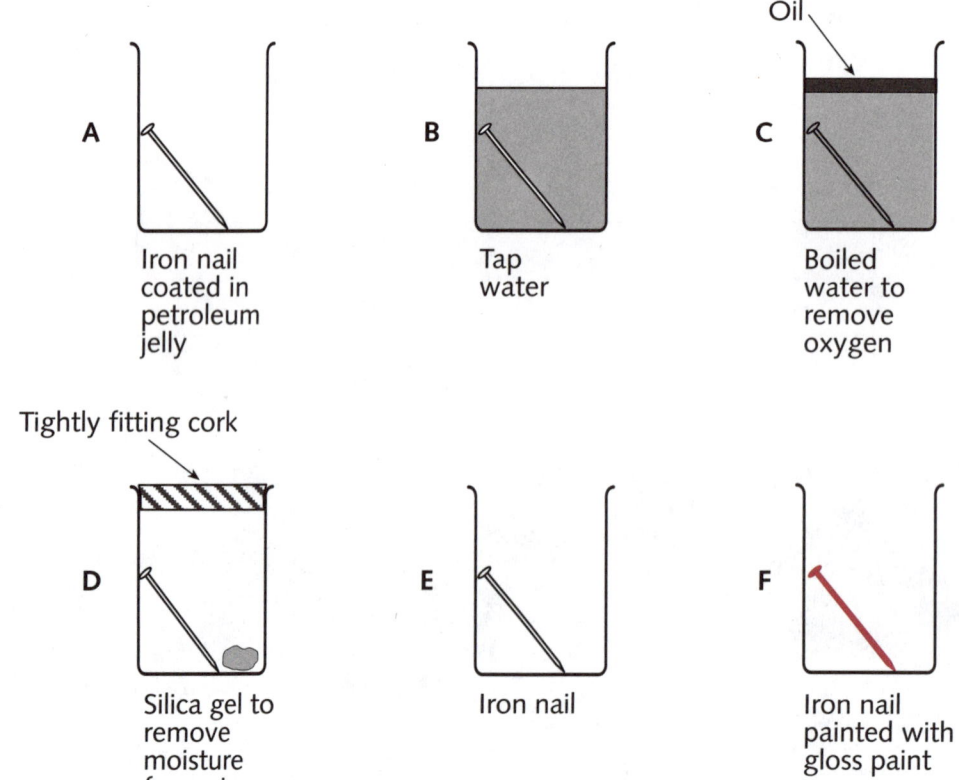

A
Iron nail coated in petroleum jelly

B
Tap water

Oil
C
Boiled water to remove oxygen

Tightly fitting cork
D
Silica gel to remove moisture from air

E
Iron nail

F
Iron nail painted with gloss paint

 **Materials**

He recorded his results after one week.

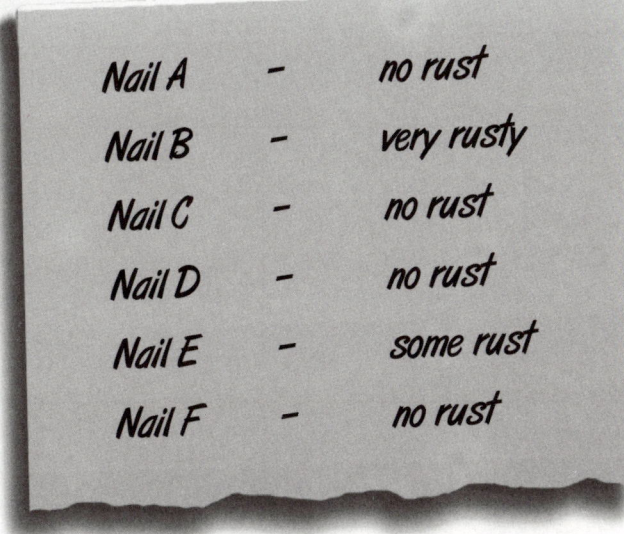

Nail A   –   no rust

Nail B   –   very rusty

Nail C   –   no rust

Nail D   –   no rust

Nail E   –   some rust

Nail F   –   no rust

a   **Use his results to help you to complete this word equation.**

iron + [   ] + [   ] ⟶ rust

b   **Name the chemical process which causes the nail to rust.**

_____

c   **Suggest the *best* way for Sandeep to stop his bike frame from rusting.**

_____

_____

PAGE
TOTAL

Changes of state

5 Read the properties listed below.

a   **Tick one or more boxes to show whether the properties describe a *solid*, a *liquid* or a *gas*.**

Property	Solid	Liquid	Gas
Particles are strongly attracted to each other			
Particles are not in a regular pattern			
Particles move far apart rapidly			
Particles vibrate about a fixed position			
Particles can *easily* be compressed			
Particles move			

Some children measured the length of a metal rod at different temperatures and recorded their results on a graph.

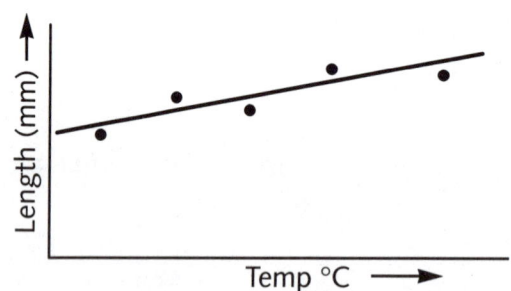

b   **Tick boxes to say what happened to the particles in the metal rod as its temperature increased.**

	Decreased	Increased	Stayed the same
Size of particles			
Distance between particles			
Movement			

PAGE TOTAL

| Time started | : |
| Time finished | : |

• Test 5 •

Chemical reactions

LEVEL 6

1 Sulphuric acid reacts with iron to produce iron sulphate and hydrogen.

a Name one *metal* mentioned above.

_____

b Name two *compounds* mentioned above.

_____

c Name three *elements* present in iron sulphate.

_____

d Complete the word equation for the reaction above.

[   ] **+** [   ] ➡ [   ] **+** [   ]

e Describe a test you could carry out to prove the presence of hydrogen.

_____

_____

_____

f Write a word equation to describe what happens when:

i)   a metal carbonate reacts with an acid.

_____

ii)   a metal burns in oxygen.

_____

iii) a metal oxide reacts with acid.

_____

PAGE TOTAL

Sound

2

Jack is playing his guitar.
The oscilloscope shows a trace for the sound produced when he plucks a string.

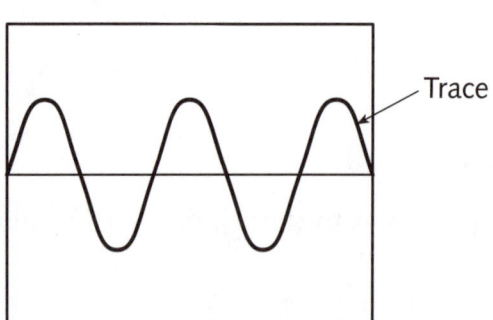

Trace

a   **Draw two arrows on the diagram above and label each to show:**

i)   the *amplitude* of the sound (label as A)

ii)   the *wavelength* of the sound (label as W)

PAGE
TOTAL

 *Sound*

He tightens the string and plucks it in the same way.

higher   **softer**

louder   **pitch**

amplitude   **lower**

b **Choose two of the words above to complete these sentences:**

The sound is _____ than before. The _____ of the sound has changed.

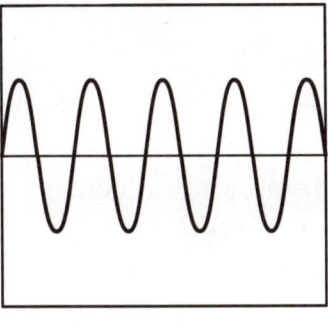

i)

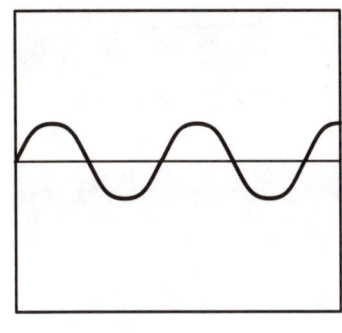

ii)

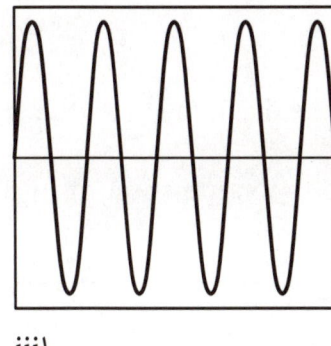

iii)

c **Which trace shows the sound he hears now – i, ii, or iii?**

_____

d **Which trace shows the loudest sound – i, ii, or iii?**

_____

Listening to loud music for long periods of time may permanently damage your hearing.

e **What frequency of sound are you less likely to hear if this happens?**

_____

_____

PAGE
TOTAL

Cell structure

3

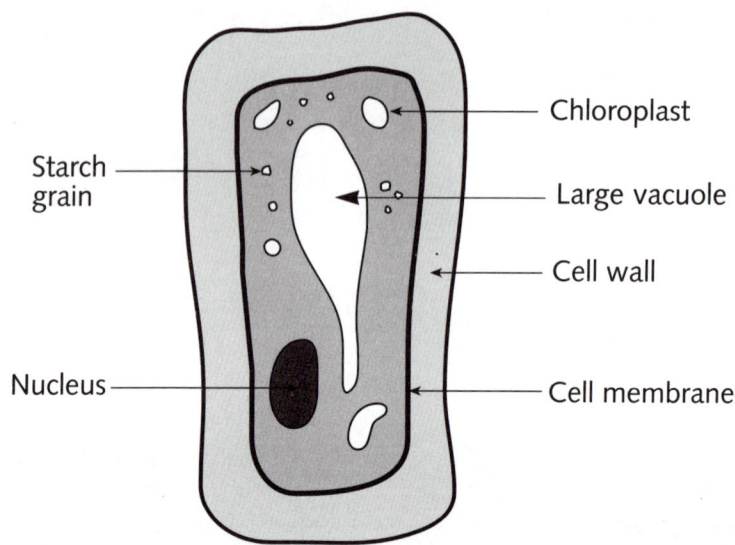

Starch grain

Nucleus

Chloroplast

Large vacuole

Cell wall

Cell membrane

The diagram shows the structure of a leaf cell.

a   **Name three things that are in a plant cell but not in an animal cell.**

_____

_____

_____

b   **Explain why the cell in the diagram could not have come from the root.**

_____

_____

c   Plants differ from animals in that they make their own food.

i)   **What is this process called?**

_____

ii)   **What part of the cell is necessary for food production?**

_____

PAGE TOTAL

■■■ *Cell structure*

d   Plants need light to make food.

> **Name two other things needed from the environment to make food.**

i)   _____   ☐

ii) _____   ☐

e   **Write a word equation to show what happens during food production in the plant.**

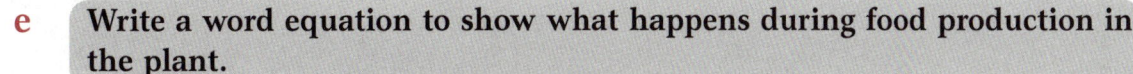

☐

f   **Name three ways in which the rubber plant's leaves are adapted to produce food.**

i)   _____   ☐

ii) _____   ☐

iii) _____   ☐

PAGE TOTAL

Health

4

Government Warning!

Tobacco seriously damages health.
Smoking when pregnant
can harm your baby.

a   Cigarette smoke contains various substances that are harmful to health. *Carbon monoxide* is one. It is a poisonous gas which is absorbed 300 times more readily into the blood stream than oxygen.

Name the two other main harmful substances in cigarette smoke.

i)   _____

ii)   _____

b   Many people find it difficult to give up smoking, even though they know it may kill them. They have become *addicted* to a very powerful drug.

Name this drug:

_____

c   Name one main substance in cigarette smoke that can cause cancer:

_____

PAGE
TOTAL

 Health

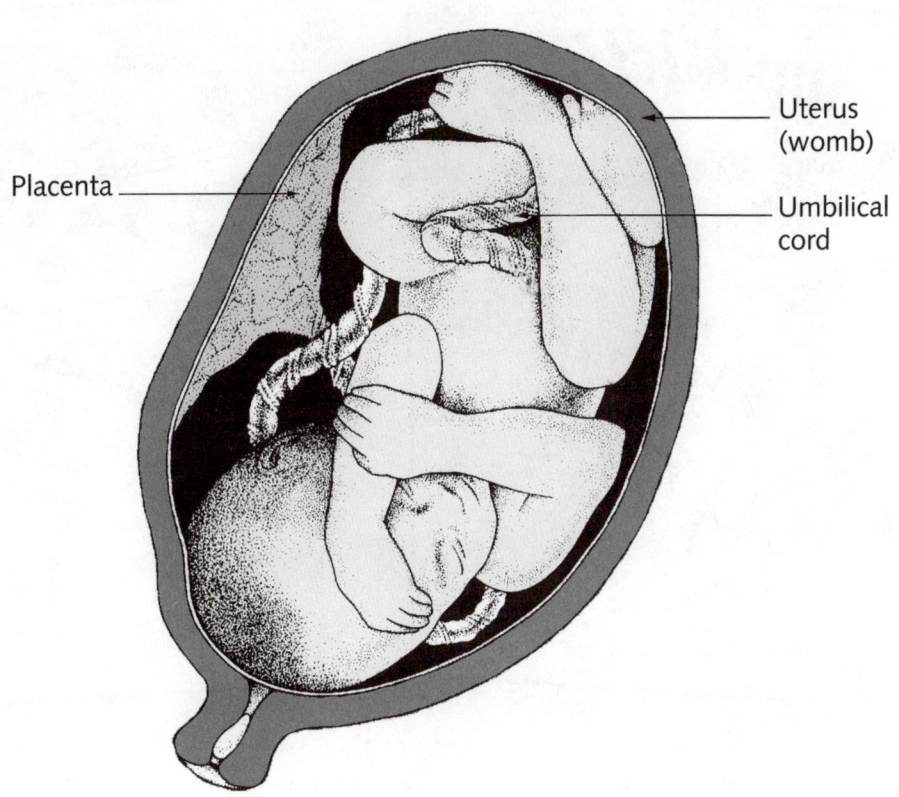

Placenta

Uterus (womb)

Umbilical cord

d   The diagram shows a foetus in the womb.

Explain how SMOKING WHEN PREGNANT CAN HARM YOUR BABY.

_____

_____

_____

_____

PAGE TOTAL

Coloured light

5

Alan has designed a card for Heather. He has made two pairs of spectacles with different coloured lenses.

a   She looks at her card through the *red lenses.*

Describe what happens to:

i)   the red flowers _____

ii)   the blue pot _____

iii)   the green leaves _____

b   She looks at her card through the *yellow lenses.*

Describe what happens to:

i)   the green leaves _____

ii)   the red flowers _____

PAGE TOTAL

Energy transfer

6

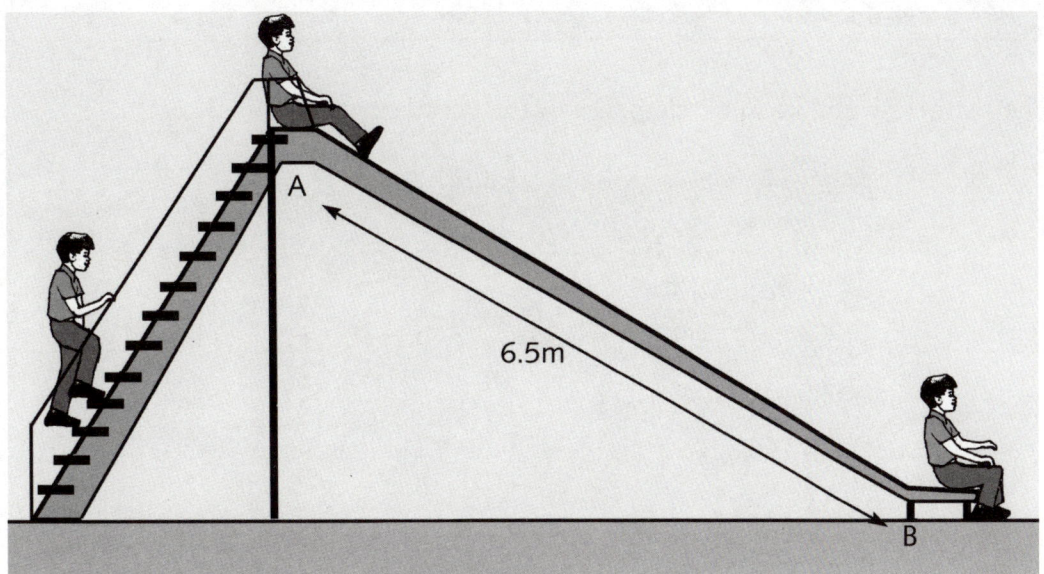

Joe climbs to the top of the ladder.

a   **What type of energy has he gained?**

_____

b   As he accelerates down the slippery slide, most of the energy he had gained is converted into another type of energy.

Name this other type of energy.

_____

c   **By the time Joe stops the energy has been converted again. What type of energy has it been converted into?**

_____

d   **What caused this conversion of energy?**

_____

e   The slide measures 6.5 metres. Joe takes 5 secs to travel from A to B.

What is his average speed as he travels from A to B?

_____

PAGE TOTAL

Time started	:
Time finished	:

• **Test 6** •

Chemical Reactions

LEVEL 7

1 The list below shows some elements in the reactivity series.

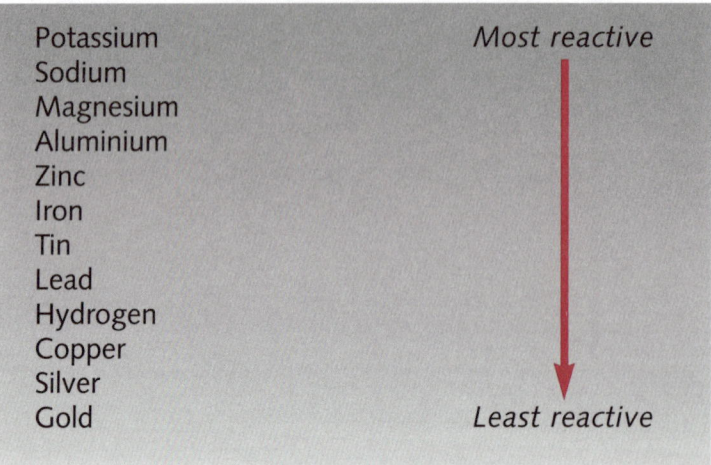

Potassium — *Most reactive*
Sodium
Magnesium
Aluminium
Zinc
Iron
Tin
Lead
Hydrogen
Copper
Silver
Gold — *Least reactive*

When iron filings are added to a copper sulphate solution, the iron *displaces* the copper and iron sulphate and copper are produced.

a   **Use this information to predict what, if anything, will happen when:**

i)   Magnesium is added to a solution of zinc sulphate.

_____

ii)   Lead is added to a solution of copper nitrate.

_____

iii) Copper is added to dilute sulphuric acid.

_____

b   **Using information from the reactivity series, give one good reason why copper is used for water pipes in our homes.**

_____

c   **Write the names of the substances described by the following chemical formulae.**

i) $NaCl$ _____

ii) $CaCO_3$ _____

iii) $AgNO_3$ _____

iv) H_2SO_4 _____

PAGE TOTAL

Forces

2

John takes his daughter Joci for a walk by the river. She ignores the 'Danger' sign and sinks in the mud. John places a piece of wood over the mud. He walks along it and kneels down to rescue her.

a   **Explain why John does not sink in the mud, even though he is much heavier than Joci.**

_____

_____

_____

b   The piece of wood John uses is 1.5m long and 0.5m wide. When he stands on the wood, he exerts a pressure of 1000 Pascals.

i)   What force does John exert in Newtons?

_____

ii)   Write the equation you used to calculate the force John exerted.

_____

PAGE
TOTAL

Electromagnets

3

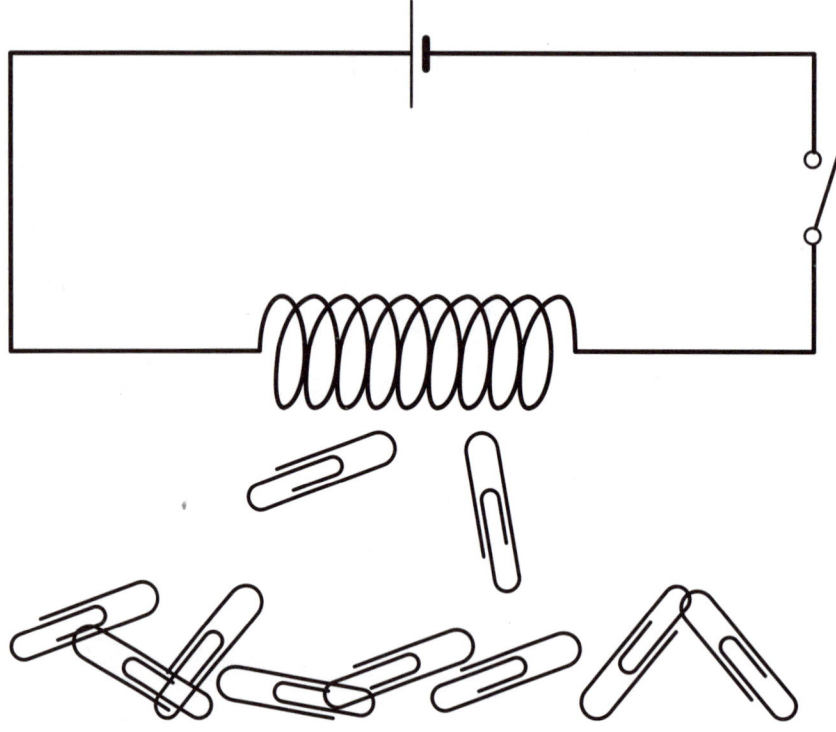

Jacqui and Gavin are constructing an electromagnet.
They close the switch.
The two paper clips nearest to the electromagnet are attracted to it.

a   **Suggest three ways in which they could make their electromagnet stronger.**

i) _____

_____

ii) _____

_____

iii) _____

_____

PAGE
TOTAL

■ ■ ■ *Electromagnets*

Electromagnets are used in fire alarms, causing them to ring continuously when the switch is closed.

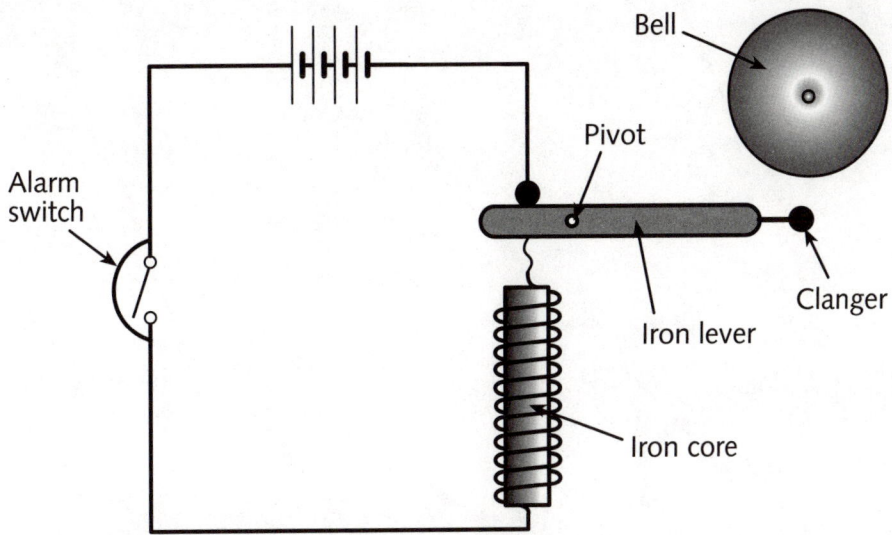

   A   The circuit is broken
   B   The electromagnet attracts the iron lever
   C   The iron lever swings away from the electromagnet
   D   The iron core becomes magnetised
   E   The bell rings
   F   The circuit is completed

b   **Use the letters A to F in the diagram below to arrange the sentences in the correct sequence to show how the fire bell rings continuously.**

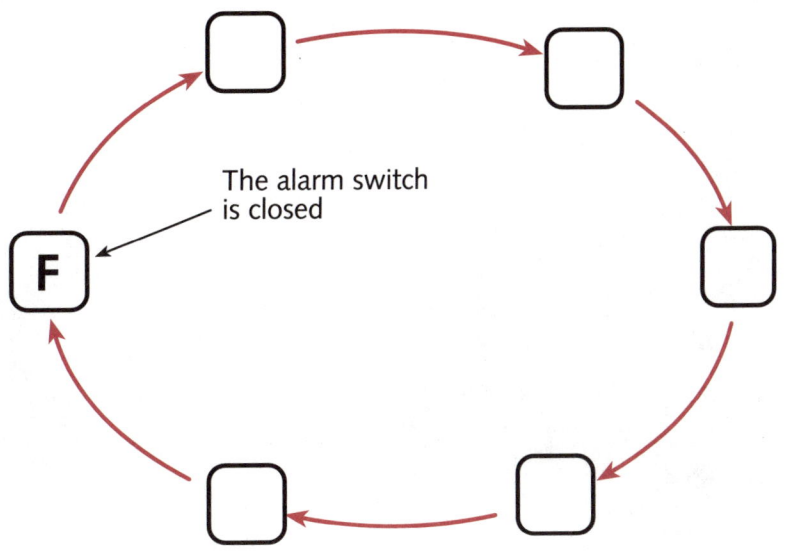

PAGE
TOTAL

Ecology

4

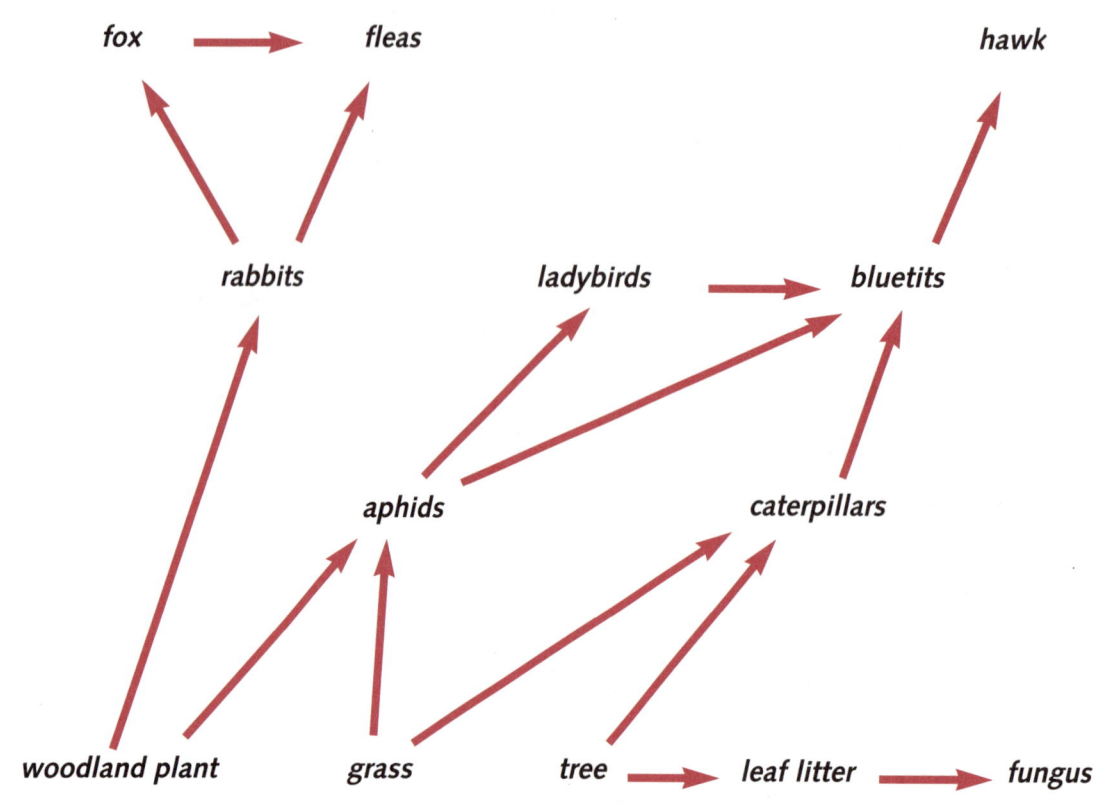

a **Use the plants or animals in this wood web to name:**

i) a producer _____ □

ii) a primary consumer _____ □

iii) a top predator _____ □

iv) a decomposer _____ □

v) a secondary consumer _____ □

▪▪▪ *Ecology*

woodland plant ➡ rabbit ➡ fox

The arrows show the flow of energy through one food chain in the food web.

b   **Give two reasons why *not all* the energy stored in the rabbit's body is transferred to the fox.**

i) _____ ☐

ii) _____ ☐

c   A, B and C show three different pyramids of numbers from the wood web.

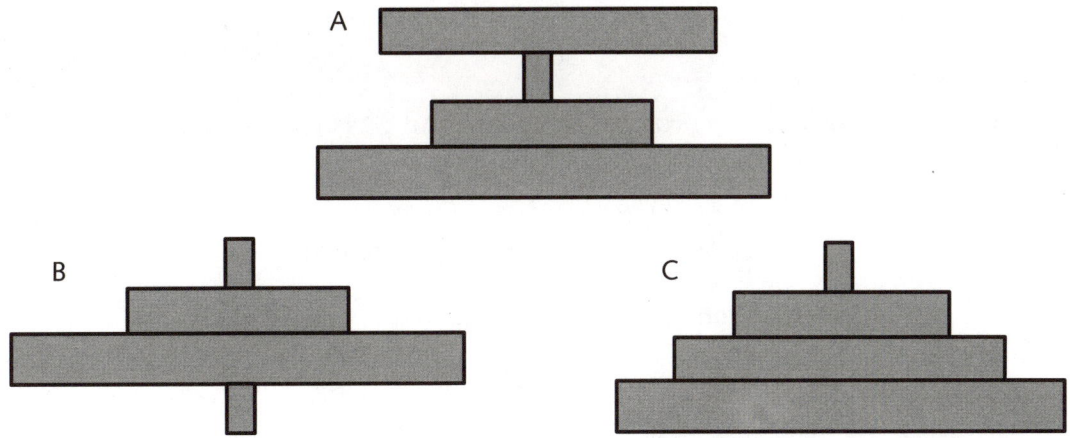

Write A, B or C beside each food chain to show which it best represents:

i)   grass ➡ caterpillars ➡ robins ➡ hawks   ☐   ☐

ii) woodland plants ➡ rabbits ➡ fox ➡ fleas   ☐   ☐

iii) tree ➡ aphids ➡ ladybirds ➡ blue tits   ☐   ☐

The human body

5 Maddy has just completed a 1500 metres race.
She has become hot and sweaty.

a **Name two other things that have happened to her as a result of running the race.**

i) _____

ii) _____

b **Choose from these words to complete the passage below.**

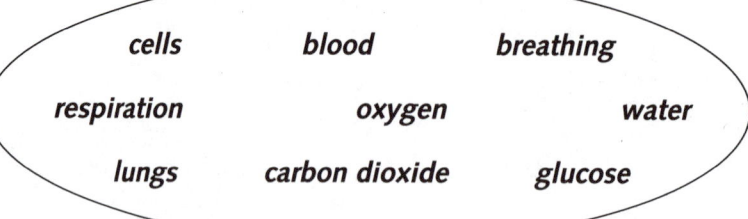

cells   blood   breathing

respiration   oxygen   water

lungs   carbon dioxide   glucose

_____ is the process that provided the energy for her to run the

race. _____ combines with _____ to release energy.

As a result _____ and _____ are produced. This

process occurred in the _____ in her body.

PAGE
TOTAL

Earth in space

6

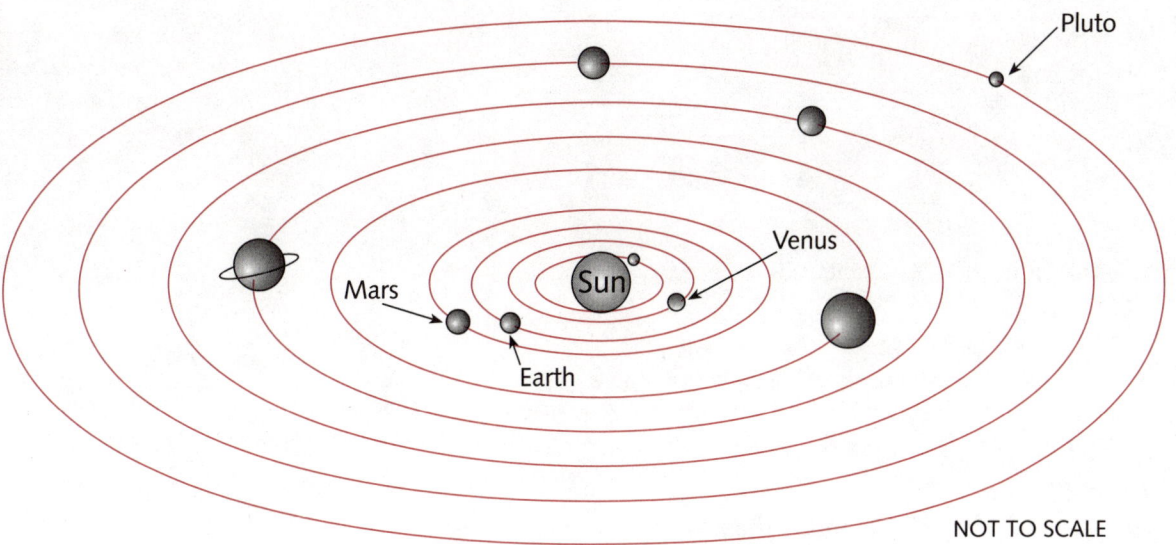

NOT TO SCALE

Four of the planets in our solar system have been named.

a   In the positions shown, one of the named planets can be seen from Earth.

> **i)   Name the planet that can be seen from Earth.**

_____   ☐

> **ii) Explain why this planet can be seen.**

_____   ☐

b   Neptune, Mercury and Uranus are three planets that have not been named.

> **Use arrows to name these planets on the diagram above.**   ☐ ☐
>   ☐

c   **What force keeps the planets in orbit around the Sun.**

_____   ☐

d   Artificial satellites have increased our knowledge of the planets and distant stars. Some have telescopes on them and are used for space research.

> **Name two other uses of artificial satellites.**

i) _____   ☐

ii) _____   ☐

• Answers to Test 1 •

1 a)

Time of measurement	Position of shadow
9.00am	C
10.30am	B
12.00 noon	A

b)

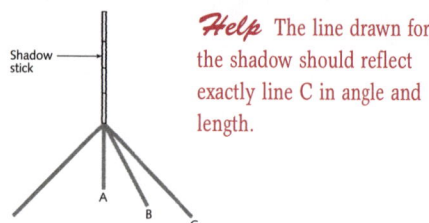

Help The line drawn for the shadow should reflect exactly line C in angle and length.

c) The Earth spins around its axis once every 24 hours.

Help As the Sun shines on the shadow stick from a different angle, it causes the shadow to change position and length.
Remember – the shadow is shortest at noon (or 13.00 B.S.T.) because the Sun is highest in the sky. The apparent path the Sun takes in the sky forms a symmetrical arc – the highest point is at noon.

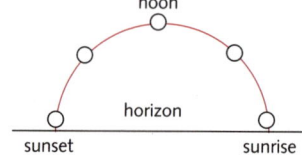

d) south

e) opaque;   straight;   cannot;   shadow.

Help You must use the word **opaque**, not solid. Some solid materials, e.g. clear plastic, allow light to travel through it and are **transparent**. Tissue paper allows **some** light to pass through, though we cannot see through it clearly. It is **translucent**. Make sure you use these words correctly.

2 a)

	Red Litmus	Blue Litmus	Acid/Alkali/Neutral
shower gel (with pH 5.5)	stays red	turns red	acid
pure water	stays red	stays blue	neutral
liquid soap	turns blue	stays blue	alkali
bathroom cleaner with limescale remover.	stays red	turns red	acid

Help Be sure you know how the pH scale works. Pure water is neutral (neither acid nor alkali) and has a pH value of 7. The lower the number, the more acid a substance is, the higher the number, the more alkaline it is.

b) neutralisation

Help Using correct scientific vocabulary is important. Your science books should contain a glossary, which gives the 'scientific' meaning of words. Use a **glossary** if you are unsure of some of the terms used in this book rather than a dictionary, which gives common usage of words. You need to know the names of different types of **reactions**, e.g. neutralisation. Other types of reaction you may need to revise are: combustion, corrosion, decomposition, displacement, oxidation, reduction.

c)

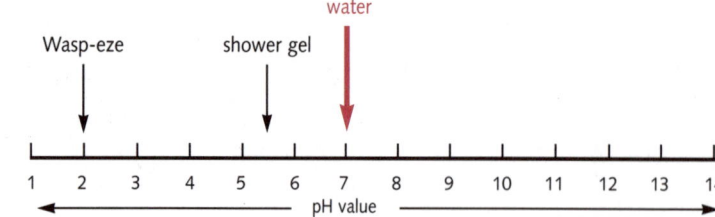

d) It is alkaline.

e) It only tells you whether a substance is acid or alkali – it doesn't show how acid or how alkaline a substance is. (Also some substances, e.g. chlorine gas, bleach the litmus.)

f) It gives a pH value/It tells you how acid/alkaline a substance is.

• 54 •

3 a)

Part of the plant	Letter
sepal	A
petal	B
fruit	D
root	E
stigma	F
anther	C
ovary	G

b)

Part of plant	Function
petal	produces male cell
stigma	attracts insects
sepal	absorbs water and minerals
ovary	protects developing flower
leaf	grows into new plant
root	receives pollen
anther	produces female cell
seed	makes food

c) **i)** When an insect visits a flower, ____pollen____ is deposited on the

__stigma (or carpel)__ . This is known as ____pollination____ .

ii) The pollen grain may grow a tube down to the ovary.

The ____male____ cell passes down the tube and fuses with the

____female____ cell. This is known as ____fertilisation____ .

Help Read the answer carefully and make sure you understand the difference between pollination and fertilisation.

4 a) duckweed → tadpoles → water beetles → pike

Help Remember arrows in the food chain mean 'is eaten by'. They also show the direction of the energy transfer.

b) (i) duckweed   (ii) tadpoles   (iii) water beetle or pike

c) The number of the tadpoles would decrease.

Help Fewer pike would mean that there would be more water beetles to eat the tadpoles.

5 **a)**

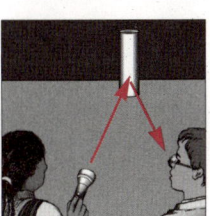

Help Remember light travels in straight lines. We see things because light travels from the source (the torch in this case), and 'bounces off' or is **reflected** from the object and enters our eyes. Make sure the arrows you have drawn show this.

b)

ii) position B

Help When light is reflected off a shiny surface, the **angle of reflection** is equal to the **angle of incidence** (the angle at which it hits the mirror). We always measure the angles in relation to the norm, which is perpendicular to the surface.

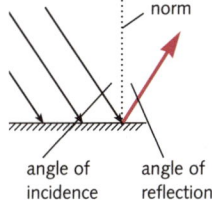

angle of incidence   angle of reflection

c) **(i)**   **(ii)**

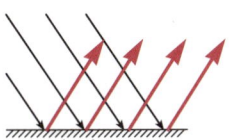

Smooth surface (mirror)

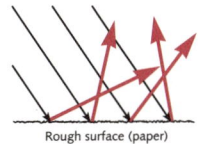

Rough surface (paper)

Help The same rule applies here as above, but in the rough surface the 'norm' doesn't follow a regular pattern.

TOTAL MARKS FOR TEST 1 = 45
25 or less = Lots to do!   26 to 37 = Revise your weak spots...   38+ = Well Done! Now move on

Answers to Test 2

1 a)

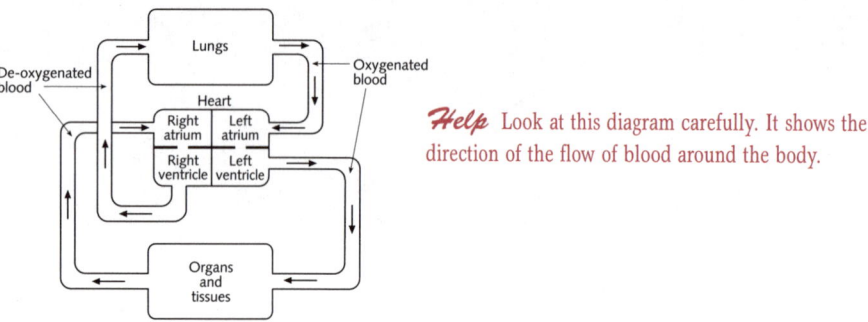

Help Look at this diagram carefully. It shows the direction of the flow of blood around the body.

The diagram shows the _____circulatory_____ system in the human body.

The right side of the heart receives _____de-oxygenated_____ blood and pumps

it to the _____lungs_____ .

The left side of the heart pumps _____oxygenated_____ blood to the

organs and tissues/rest of body.

_____Veins_____ carry blood to the heart.

b) One from each of these:

(i) transports useful substances (e.g. digested food/glucose, hormones, water, vitamins), transports oxygen/carbon dioxide

(ii) fights disease/kills viruses + bacteria

2 a)

	It melts first
	It is sweeter
✓	It dissolves more easily
	It disappears the quickest

b) (i) type of sugar;   (ii) number of stirs

c) Any three of these: temperature of water/type and size of container/amount of sugar/volume of water added

Help Remember, using correct scientific vocabulary is essential when answering test questions.

d) We sprinkled the sugar (the _____solute_____) into the tea (the _____solvent_____)

to form a _____solution_____ . The sugar _____dissolved_____ .

We concluded that caster sugar was more _____soluble_____ in tea than

granulated sugar.

Help Check the words in a glossary if you got any wrong or guessed right!

3 a)

	(i)		(ii)		(iii)	
Red	Ⓡ	✓	Ⓡ	☐	1	☐
Amber	Ⓐ	✓	Ⓐ	☐	2	✓
Green	Ⓖ	☐	Ⓖ	☐	3	✓
					4	☐

b)

How to make the traffic lights work *Close the switches shown*				
	1	2	3	4
Ⓡ	✓	✓		
Ⓡ + Ⓐ	✓	✓	✓	
Ⓖ	✓			✓
Ⓐ	✓		✓	

Help A complete circuit is needed for electricity to flow and the lamps to shine. Opening switches breaks the circuit.
When you revise **electricity** make sure:
• you have revised all the **symbols** you have been taught and can use them **to draw circuits**.
• you know the **units for measurement** of voltage, current, resistance, and how they are **measured/changed**.
• you have included **electric charge and static electricity** in your revision.
When you revise **magnetism** make sure:
• you include **magnetic fields** and **patterns caused by magnetic forces** around the magnet.

4 a)

	Light	Sound
Travel through air	✓	✓
Travel through a vacuum	✓	
Travel through wood		✓
Travel through water	✓	✓
Travel in all directions from a source	✓	✓
Can be reflected off hard surfaces	✓	✓

Note Both Light and Sound boxes must be correct to gain one mark.

b) Light travels faster than sound.

c) (i)

The thunder is quieter than before	
The thunder is louder than before	✓
The thunder sounds the same	

(ii) The storm is getting closer.

5 a) A no legs; B wings; C no wings; D no shell
b) A lime; B ash; C sycamore; D horse chestnut; E beech; F oak

Make sure you understand all the correct answers in these tests before going on to do the more difficult tests 3 and 4.
Revise if you are still unsure.

TOTAL MARKS FOR TEST 2 = 45
25 or less = Lots to do!   26 to 37 = Revise your weak spots...   38+ = Well Done! Now move on

• Answers to Test 3 •

1 (i) Use a magnet *Help* Steel is magnetic; aluminium is not.

(ii) Sieve *Help* Choose a sieve which allows only the sand to pass through.

(iii) Chromatography

Help Chromatographic paper allows pigments to travel along it. Each pigment travels at a different speed so separating them out.

(iv) Distillation

Help Boil the solution to evaporate the water, leaving salt behind, collect vapour and cool. It condenses to form water.

(v) Add water to mixture, filter and distil.

Help The insoluble powder will remain in the filter paper. The second powder can be separated by distillation (as iv).

(vi) Allow layers of liquid to separate and decant.

Help Remove top layer carefully by suction/using a pipette/using a separating funnel. Decant layers into separate containers.
Key words in this question that you must be familiar with are: chromatography, distillation, evaporation, condensation, insoluble, soluble, immiscible.

2

Definitely inherited	Definitely environmental	Both environmental and inherited
brown eyes long nose	London accent loves to wear designer-label clothes	slim 1.6m tall intelligent excellent cyclist freckles

Help Freckles are environmental as well as inherited, because hot sun increases their size and numbers.

3 a) $365\frac{1}{4}$

Help Remember, every fourth year is a leap year and has one extra day, Feb 29th, which accounts for the extra quarters.

b) **c)**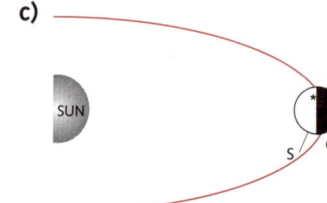

Help When viewed from the north pole, the Earth spins on its axis in an **anti-clockwise** direction, so in question c) Britain is just approaching darkness (17.00) hours.

d) 1700 hours   **e) (i)** summer   **(ii)** The Earth is tilted on its axis.

4 a) **A** mouth   **B** oesophagus   **C** stomach   **D** small intestine   **E** large intestine   **F** anus

b)

Function	Part of digestive system
Absorbs water from undigested food	E
Transports food to the stomach	B
Absorbs digested food into the blood	D
Starch starts to be broken down	A
Undigested food is expelled	F
Protein starts to be broken down	C

Help You need to revise the **names** of all the main body parts and organ systems for **level 4**. You need to revise the **function** of the circulatory, digestive, reproductive and respiratory systems for **level 5**.

5 a) & b)

Source of energy	Column 1 renewable	Column 2 non-renewable	Column 3 Sun is original source of energy
solar	✓		✓
wind	✓		✓
coal		✓	✓
gas		✓	✓
nuclear		✓	
oil		✓	✓
hydro-electricity	✓		✓

TOTAL MARKS FOR TEST 3 = 45
25 or less = Lots to do!   26 to 37 = Revise your weak spots...   38+ = Well Done! Now move on

• Answers to Test 4 •

1 a) **A** igneous   **B** metamorphic   **C** sedimentary   **D** sedimentary   **E** igneous

b) sample C   **c)** (i) pressure   (ii) heat

d) (i) X

(ii) The magma/molten lava cooled more slowly at position X than at Y or Z. The slower the magma cools, the larger the crystals./There isn't any magma/molten lava in this position.

2 a) (i)

(ii) because he is accelerating/ speeding up

b) (i)

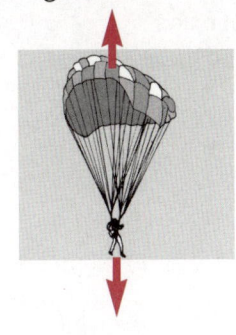

(ii) gravity

(iii) friction/air resistance

c)

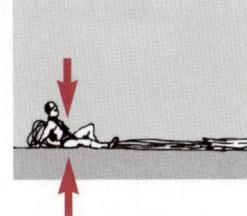

3 a) vitamins   **b)** Any two of these: chicken/nuts/egg

c) Any one of these: It prevents constipation/It keeps food moving/It may help to prevent bowel cancer.

d) Any three of these: brown rice/nuts/peas/red peppers/spring onions

e)

Food type	Use to the body
carbohydrates	provides energy
protein	for growth and repair
fat	storing energy

Help Make sure you know the role of all the main food types that ensure good health.

4 a)

iron + | oxygen/air | + | water | ➡ rust

b) oxidation/corrosion   **c)** paint it

Help When writing an equation, the reactants are always on the left and the product(s) on the right. Remember this for questions in future tests.

5 a)

Property	Solid	Liquid	Gas
Particles are strongly attracted to each other	✓		
Particles are not in a regular pattern		✓	✓
Particles move far apart rapidly			✓
Particles vibrate about a fixed position	✓		
Particles can *easily* be compressed			✓
Particles move	✓	✓	✓

Help You must know about the arrangement and movement of particles in solids, liquids and gases. This will help you understand why they behave differently.

b)

Increased	Decreased	Increased	Stayed the same
Size of particles			✓
Distance between particles		✓	
Movement		✓	

Make sure you understand all the correct answers in these tests before going on to do the more difficult tests: Tests 5 and 6. Revise if you are still unsure.

TOTAL MARKS FOR TEST 4 = 45

25 or less = Lots to do!   26 to 37 = Revise your weak spots...   38+ = Well Done! Now move on

• Answers to Test 5 •

1 a) iron   **b)** sulphuric acid, iron sulphate   **c)** iron, sulphur, oxygen

  d) | sulphuric acid | + | iron | ➡ | iron sulphate | + | hydrogen |

  e) Add a lighted splint. If hydrogen is present, a 'pop' will occur. *Help* This is caused by the hydrogen burning.

  f) (i) metal carbonate + acid → metal salt + carbon dioxide + water

    (ii) metal + oxygen → metal oxide

    (iii) metal oxide + acid → metal salt + water

2 a) 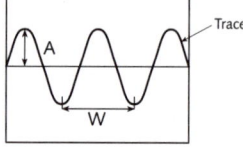   **b)** higher;   pitch

    c) (i)

    d) (iii)

    e) higher frequency sounds/high pitched sounds

3 a) Any three of these: cell wall/large vacuole/chloroplast/starch grain

  b) It contains chloroplasts.   **c)** (i) photosynthesis   (ii) chloroplasts

  d) (i) carbon dioxide   (ii) water

  e) | carbon dioxide | + | water | ➡ | glucose/sugar | + | oxygen |

  f) Any three of these:

    (i) Large surface area traps sunlight.

    (ii) Veins transport water from roots.

    (iii) Can turn to face sunlight.

    (iv) Stomata – which open and close to control loss of water during transpiration.

    (v) Contains chloroplasts.

4 a) (i) nicotine   (ii) tar   **b)** nicotine   **c)** tar

  d) Any one of these:

  A smoking mother's blood carries less oxygen than a non-smoker because carbon monoxide has been absorbed instead.

  The baby might not receive enough oxygen necessary for healthy growth.

  Poisonous substances produced in cigarette smoke can pass from the mother's to the baby's blood.

5 a) (i) They will not be seen/They disappear.   **b)** (i) They look green.

    (ii) It looks black.   (ii) They look red.

    (iii) They look black.

6 a) potential/gravitational energy   **b)** kinetic/movement energy

  c) heat energy   **d)** friction

  e) 1.3 m/sec (N.B. units m/sec must be given.)

TOTAL MARKS FOR TEST 5 = 45
25 or less = Lots to do!   26 to 37 = Revise your weak spots...   38+ = Well Done! Now move on

• Answers to Test 6 •

1 a) (i) Magnesium sulphate and zinc will be produced (magnesium displaces zinc).

(ii) Lead nitrate and copper will be produced (lead displaces copper).

(iii) No reaction will occur.

Help Remember, any metal will displace another lower than it in the reactivity series.

b) Copper does not react with water.

c) (i) sodium chloride   (ii) calcium carbonate   (iii) silver nitrate   (iv) sulphuric acid

2 a) The plank of wood has a greater surface area than John (or Joci's) feet. His weight is spread out over a greater area. The pressure he exerts is greatly reduced and so he does not sink into the mud.

b) (i) 750N   (ii) Force = Pressure × Area

3 a) (i) Increase the number of batteries/voltage/current.

(ii) Increase the number of coils/turns in the wire.

(iii) Insert an iron nail/rod in the coil.

b)

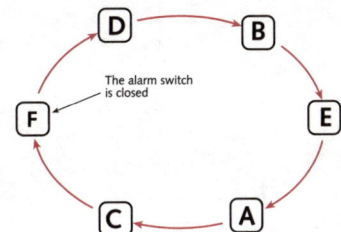

Help When you revise **electricity** and **magnetism** make sure you know:

• all the **symbols** you have been taught and can use them to draw circuits;

• the units of measurement for **voltage, current and resistance**;

• about **electric charge** and **static electricity**;

• **magnetic fields** and **patterns caused by magnetic forces** around the magnet.

4 a) Any one of these: (i) woodland plant/grass/tree/leaf litter   (ii) rabbit/aphid/caterpillar

(iii) hawk/fox   (iv) fungus   (v) ladybird/blue tit/fox/fleas

b) (i) Some energy is lost as heat/during metabolism/respiration.

(ii) Some energy is used for growth/repair.

c) (i) C   (ii) A   (ii) B

5 a) (i) She is breathing more quickly.

(ii) Her pulse rate has increased/heart is beating faster.

b) respiration;   oxygen/glucose;   glucose/oxygen;   carbon dioxide/water;   water/carbon dioxide;

cells *Help* Be clear about the difference between **respiration** and **breathing**.

6 a) (i) Mars   (ii) It reflects the Sun's light and can be seen on a clear night.

b)

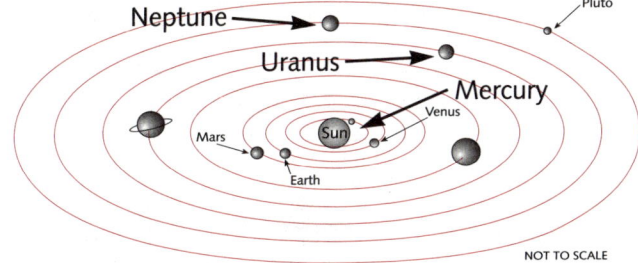

NOT TO SCALE

c)   gravity/gravitational force of attraction between the Sun and planets

d)   Any two of these: spying/navigation/monitoring weather/communication, e.g. TV/phone/radio.

TOTAL MARKS FOR TEST 6 = 45

25 or less = Lots to do!   26 to 37 = Revise your weak spots...   38+ = Well Done! Genius!

• Revision Index •

	Levels 4–5 Test 1	Levels 4–5 Test 2	Levels 5–6 Test 3	Levels 5–6 Test 4	Levels 6–7 Test 5	Levels 6–7 Test 6
Life processes and living things						
LIFE PROCESSES AND CELL ACTIVITY	③		④		③	
HUMANS AS ORGANISMS						
nutrition and digestion			④	③		
circulation		①				
movement						
reproduction					④	
breathing						
respiration						⑤
health					④	
GREEN PLANTS AS ORGANISMS						
nutrition and growth					③	
reproduction	③					
respiration						
VARIATION, CLASSIFICATION AND INHERITANCE						
variation			②			
classification		⑤				
inheritance			②			
LIVING THINGS IN THEIR ENVIRONMENT						
adaptation					③	
feeding relationships	④					④
competition	④					
Materials and their properties						
CLASSIFYING MATERIALS						
solids, liquids, gases				⑤		
elements						①
compounds						①
mixtures			①			
metals and non-metals					①	

• Revision Index •

	Levels 4–5 Test 1	Levels 4–5 Test 2	Levels 5–6 Test 3	Levels 5–6 Test 4	Levels 6–7 Test 5	Levels 6–7 Test 6
CHANGING MATERIALS						
physical changes		②				
geological changes				①		
chemical reactions				④	①	①
PATTERNS OF BEHAVIOUR						
metals					①	①
acids and bases	②				①	

Physical processes

	Levels 4–5 Test 1	Levels 4–5 Test 2	Levels 5–6 Test 3	Levels 5–6 Test 4	Levels 6–7 Test 5	Levels 6–7 Test 6
ELECTRICITY		③				③
MAGNETISM						③
FORCES AND MOTION						
force and linear motion				②	⑥	
force and pressure						②
LIGHT AND SOUND						
the behaviour of light	① ⑤	④			⑤	
hearing					②	
vibration and sound		④			②	
THE EARTH AND BEYOND						
the solar system	①		③			⑥
ENERGY RESOURCES AND ENERGY TRANSFER						
energy resources			⑤			
conservation of energy					⑥	④

This chart shows the main topics in the National Curriculum which are tested at Key Stage 3.

The number in the circle, for example ⑤, refers to the number of the question which assesses the topic.

Tick each topic as you complete the tests and show how successful you were.

Use the chart to:

1 find the topics you want
2 check the level of each question
3 identify your strengths and weaknesses
4 plan your revision

Achievement record

When you complete each pair of tests – Tests 1 and 2, Tests 3 and 4, Tests 5 and 6:
- add your scores together in the boxes provided at the bottom of the page;
- record your total on the appropriate 0 to 90 mark scale below.

You can now see the National Curriculum level you have achieved in each pair of tests.

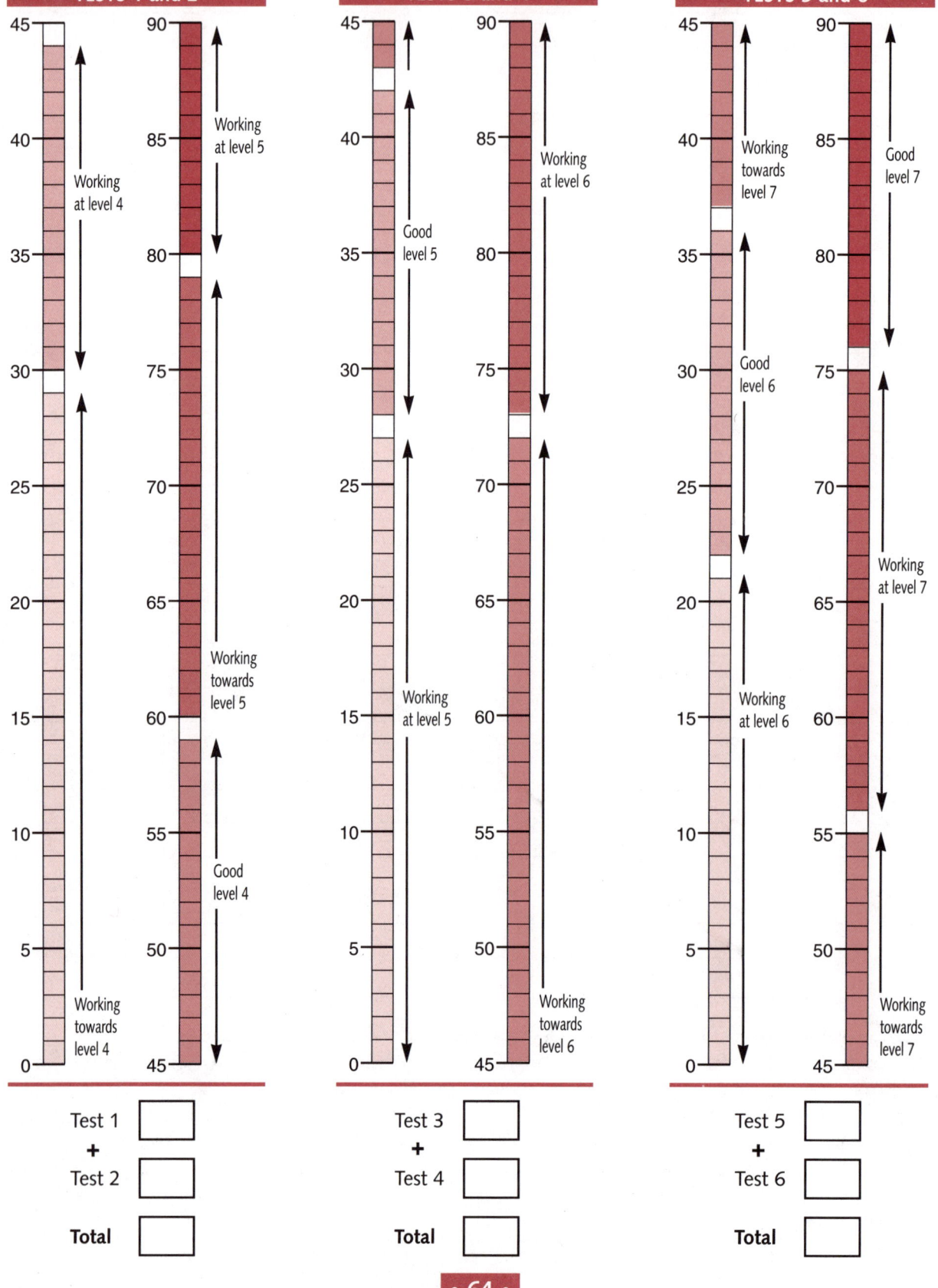

TESTS 1 and 2	TESTS 3 and 4	TESTS 5 and 6

TESTS 1 and 2

- Working at level 4
- Working at level 5
- Working towards level 5
- Good level 4
- Working towards level 4

TESTS 3 and 4

- Good level 5
- Working at level 6
- Working at level 5
- Working towards level 6

TESTS 5 and 6

- Working towards level 7
- Good level 7
- Good level 6
- Working at level 7
- Working at level 6
- Working towards level 7

Test 1 ☐
+
Test 2 ☐

Total ☐

Test 3 ☐
+
Test 4 ☐

Total ☐

Test 5 ☐
+
Test 6 ☐

Total ☐